CANADA

IN TRANSITION

edited by GRANT S. McCLELLAN
Editor, *Current Magazine*

THE REFERENCE SHELF

Volume 49   Number 1

THE H. W. WILSON COMPANY

New York   1977

THE REFERENCE SHELF

The books in this series contain reprints of articles, excerpts from books, and addresses on current issues and social trends in the United States and other countries. There are six separately bound numbers in each volume, all of which are generally published in the same calendar year. One number is a collection of recent speeches; each of the others is devoted to a single subject and gives background information and discussion from various points of view, concluding with a comprehensive bibliography. Books in the series may be purchased individually or on subscription.

Copyright © 1977

By The H. W. Wilson Company

PRINTED IN THE UNITED STATES OF AMERICA

Library of Congress Cataloging in Publication Data
Main entry under title:

Canada in transition.

(The Reference shelf ; v. 49, no. 1)
Bibliography: p.
SUMMARY: A series of articles dealing with the changing economic, political, and social aspects of present-day Canada and the influence of an emerging spirit of nationalism.
1. Canada—Politics and government—1945-   Addresses, essays, lectures. 2. Canada—Economic conditions—1945-   Addresses, essays, lectures. 3. Canada—Foreign relations—1945-   Addresses, essays, lectures. 4. Québec (Province)—History—Autonomy and independence movements—Addresses, essays, lectures. [1. Canada—Politics and government —1945-   Addresses, essays, lectures. 2. Canada—Economic conditions —1945-   Addresses, essays, lectures. 3. Canada—Foreign relations—1945-   Addresses, essays, lectures. 4. Québec (Province)—History—Autonomy and independence movements—Addresses, essays, lectures]
I. McClellan, Grant S.   II. Series.
F1034.2.C29   320.9'71'064   77-951
ISBN 0-8242-0603-7

PREFACE

Any study of Canada in the 1970s must take into account the emergence of the strong spirit of nationalism that is affecting all facets of Canadian life. Once satisfied to prosper under the protection and guidance of its two "natural" allies—Great Britain first, and later the United States—Canada is now following a course of its own choosing, in the strong belief that Canadian priorities, and not those of any other nation, should be the main determinants of national policies.

The repercussions of such policies are more acutely felt in the United States than elsewhere in the world for the simple reason that the ties that bind Canada to the United States are tighter than those to any other nation. Thus, as Canada has begun to shrug off some of the influence of foreigners on its policies, the United States has been the first to experience the shock waves.

And shock waves there have been. Canada in recent years has enacted legislation restricting foreign (i.e., American) publishing and broadcast rights in the country in an attempt to restore balance between the American companies and their Canadian counterparts. Economically, there are now laws on both the federal and provincial level that bar any foreign investment in Canada that is not of "significant benefit" to the Canadian people. And politically, Prime Minister Pierre Elliott Trudeau and his ruling Liberal Party have steered a course among nations of the world that not only does not parallel that of the United States, but at times actually opposes American policies and objectives.

This spirit of independent action has also reached down to the provincial level where, as contradictory as it may seem, a feeling of provincialism exists beside the feeling of nationalism. In no province is this more keenly demonstrated than in Quebec—where all the conflicts between English-speaking and French-speaking Canadians come to a head. The politically divisive situation has been further intensified by the November 1976 provincial elections in which René Lévesque and his Parti Québécois—the official policy of which is the secession of Quebec from the Canadian confederation—were swept into power.

While most observers of the Canadian scene do not foresee any immediate changes in the composition of Canada or in its relations with other nations, the articles in this volume strongly suggest that the Canada of fifteen years from now may be very different from the Canada of the 1970s.

The editor wishes to thank the authors and publishers of the selections that follow for permission to reprint them in this compilation.

GRANT S. McCLELLAN

January 1977

CONTENTS

V. CANADA'S FOREIGN RELATIONS

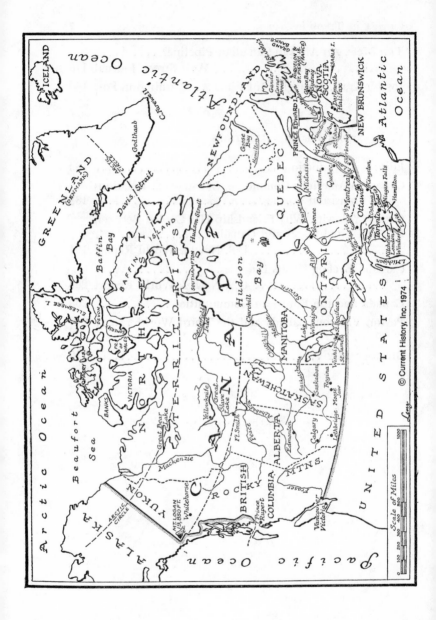

I. CANADA AND ITS IDENTITY CRISIS

EDITOR'S INTRODUCTION

Most observers of the Canadian scene agree that Canada is currently facing an identity crisis. On the one hand there is the Canada that in the last forty years has fallen under an American dominance so great that, in fact, there are almost as many things American about Canada as there are about America. On the other hand, there is the Canada that has of late been experiencing a growing sense of nationalism —a spirit that calls for the development of the Canadian features of that country's society at the expense, of course, of the American influence.

This feeling of national ambivalence is the subject of the articles in the first section of this book. The first article, by Abraham Rotstein, a Canadian teacher of political economy, is an analytical overview of this new surge of nationalism, which Rotstein says has its origin in the political and economic spheres. Gerald Clark, the editor of the Montreal *Star,* next presents us with a more detailed appraisal of how Canadian nationalism affects everyday life.

The cultural ramifications of the nationalist experience are described by the Canadian writer Mordecai Richler in the final two articles in this section. According to Richler, while a resurgence of nationalism in Canadian culture is good for the country, the outright rejection of all things American and a corresponding total acceptance of all things Canadian would prove a disservice to Canadians.

CANADA: THE NEW NATIONALISM [1]

For as long as most people can remember, a glance out of the corner of one's eye to the upper half of North America

[1] From "Canada: The New Nationalism," by Abraham Rotstein, instructor, department of political economy, University of Toronto. *Foreign Affairs.* 55:97-118. O. '76. Reprinted by permission from *Foreign Affairs,* October 1976. Copyright 1976 by Council on Foreign Relations, Inc.

would bring warm reassurance that things were moving quietly and gracefully *somewhere* in the world. Alphonse and Gaston could invariably be heard out there bowing and scraping, and toasting their long undefended border. Today, official devotees of this stately two-step are still meeting and greeting, but few take the old shuffle at face value. Instead, private conversations in directors' board rooms, in expensive lunch clubs, in government cafeterias and in faculty lounges have a distinctly worried and wary undertone.

These are not merely the nervous Nellies (American-style), or the bleeding hearts (Canadian-style). Bad consciences do exist about this overdeveloped and one-sided intimacy that has grown up between the two countries, but that, as everyone knows, is not the stuff of politics. It is not conscience and sentiment which are beginning to interfere with the work-a-day world of gas and oil and the purchase and sale of branch plants, but a new and distinct phase of Canadian nationalism.

Despite recent appearances, this nationalism is still frail and, considering the circumstances, a belated arrival on the political scene. The editor of an eminent American publication put the crucial question in a recent visit. "Why," he wanted to know, "is there so *little* nationalism in Canada?" It was clear that he knew the background very well. On the economic side, 58 percent of the manufacturing sector is in foreign hands as are 61 of the largest 102 corporations in the manufacturing, resources and utility fields. Seventy-five percent of the capital employed in our oil and natural gas industry is foreign controlled and 52 percent of the trade union movement takes orders of one sort or another from American head offices.

On the cultural side the situation is no better. About half of the university professors in the humanities and social sciences are non-Canadian. Foreign magazines account for 85 percent of the total magazine circulation; Canada still does not have its own national news weekly; foreign books (those not authored by Canadians) form 83 percent of book sales, and 71 percent of the publishing industry is foreign controlled; 96 percent of the films in Canadian cinemas are foreign, as are much of television, plays, art—and on and on it goes. In Canada, we may still own the cupboard, but little of the contents.

"Foreign," of course, means mainly American (about four-fifths) in every case. What one Canadian economist, Bruce Wilkinson, stated about Canada's intense trade concentration with the United States, can be applied to the economic and cultural situation as a whole: "Canada's position resembles more closely that of a less-developed nation than that of other developed countries."

But statistics alone do not tell the story about the quality of everyday life. It would be a mistake to evoke the image of Canada as a seething colony struggling to break loose. Canada bears rather the signs of a successful lobotomy to which it has voluntarily assented. The routine of daily existence is comfortable, decent and sane. There is only the occasional disorientation of not really knowing what country you are living in. Saunter into a drugstore and there is hardly a Canadian paperback to be found anywhere, although an enormous number have been published. The 10,000 mass paperback outlets in Canada provide the American books read by the great majority of the population, while Canadian books have their home in the 400 proper bookstores. Stroll down the main street of your average city, the marquees alight with the titles and stars of the latest films, and hardly a Canadian film is available anywhere, although several hundred have been made in recent years. Turn on your TV set and the chances are two out of three that it will be an American network show on your television screen. Silent qualms surface now and then, but soon one is lulled into passive acceptance, with a fading sense of loss. Increasingly Americanized tastes in Canada acquire a priority of their own, while the very capacity to create and relay our own sense of self rapidly atrophies.

Occasionally there are surrealistic moments that break the

numbness—untypical events that throw the "normal" situation into high relief. In the tangled skein of oil and gas negotiations between Canada and the United States, one of the landmark events occurred on September 29, 1970, when the Energy Minister Joe Greene announced that the Federal Cabinet had approved the largest gas export license in Canadian history—6.3 trillion cubic feet, to be exported over a 15-to-20-year period. The National Energy Board had urged the Cabinet to approve the massive gas export to the United States on the basis of a set of reserve figures supplied by the Canadian Petroleum Association. (Despite its name, the Association consists largely of the major American oil companies which do over 90 percent of the production and refining.) On June 2, 1971, these reserve figures were made public by the energy minister when he stated: "At 1970 rates of production, these reserves represent 923 years supply for oil and 392 years for gas."

The rest is history. In April 1975, the same National Energy Board reported that Canada would have a natural gas shortage *within this decade* and oil production would decline to the point where Canada would become a net importer of oil. Canada is already in that position. Yet the American oil companies remain undaunted and are now pressing (with Canadian government support) for the Mackenzie Valley Pipeline to carry both the Delta and Alaska gas, *because* of the urgent and imminent gas shortage.

Data on energy reserves expand and contract like an accordion but even Canadian numbness and gullibility have their limits. The rising tide of popular skepticism begins to question all the oil companies' arguments, certainly questions the basis of all our oil and gas export agreements, and even begins to wonder wistfully why oil and gas production should not be in Canadian hands.

Canada: Beginning to Come Awake

One further touch of the surreal in Canada will suffice to throw some light on the quality of everyday existence. In recent years we have had a national university commission investigating the role (actually the absence) of Canadian courses in our universities. Its recent report, *To Know Ourselves,* recounts the testimony from some American sociologists who now predominate on the staff of Canadian universities. The report states that these sociologists "were even forthright enough to tell the commission that they would not hire Canadians for 'their' departments because 'once one hires a few then they will be pushing for more and more.' "

However bizarre these episodes, the American sociologists as well as the American oil companies are, in their own way, "right." Once the game warden has declared open season, everyone is quite entitled to look to his own catch.

As a nationalist and a dispirited critic of Canadian government policy, I had no immediate answer to the question: why indeed is there so little nationalism, so little concern with serious countermeasures that are crucial to hold the American tide in check and to sustain whatever is still possible of an autonomous national existence?

For the more articulate segments of the community, the press, the political commentators, the academics and so on, it required a sophisticated myopia to fail to notice the self-immolation of Canadian independence in the postwar period. Indeed, the great American takeover has been aided and encouraged by internal forces, what one author called in a summary theme, Canada's "silent surrender." These forces are as prevalent in government as in business. They exist in the trade unions as much as in the groves of academe. The transition to institutionalized dependence occurred with the greatest impetus in the last two decades at precisely the time when, in the rest of the world, the trend was in the opposite direction.

In a belated fashion, Canada is beginning to come awake, and beginning to explore and even to implement new policies. But the penetration of American society in Canada is now so great that there is no practical way to distinguish domestic and foreign policy. New domestic policies in-

evitably touch the huge American sector closely. Official
Canadian foreign policy declarations, such as the "third
option" (the move to somewhat lesser dependence on the
United States), are little more than changing domestic policy
seen in the rearview mirror. They are an effective guide to
the past.

Thus, the future of the Canadian-American relationship
must be sought on the domestic scene but not necessarily
within the federal government. Its recent initiatives have,
on the whole, been weak. The Foreign Investment Review
Agency aims to achieve better terms for Canada on U.S.
takeovers of Canadian business and on new ventures. But
even the U.S. financial journal *Barron's* admitted: "It is
difficult to imagine a legitimate business venture which
would be impeded by the Foreign Investment Review Act
. . . the only U.S. business which wouldn't be cordially welcomed to Canada is Murder, Inc."

As far as energy is concerned, the closing of the door on
oil exports to the United States in 1982 will occur after the
horse has gone. By 1985, net imports of oil to Canada will
amount to 50 percent of Canadian requirements.

On the cultural front, the Canadian edition of *Time*
has, after a 15-year debate, been declared *non grata* because
of the ease with which dumped U.S. copy would siphon off
Canadian advertising dollars. Some additional cultural initiatives are pending.

Reassurances to Washington from the Department of External Affairs continue, but the rhetoric of officialdom in a
federal state is belied by unexpected eruptions at the pe-
riphery, somewhere in the disparate collection of regional
loyalties and semi-autonomous institutional structures which
constitute the kingdoms (in the plural) of Canada.

With little warning, gas export prices in British Columbia are hiked several times over; the province of Saskatchewan proposes to reclaim half of its potash industry now
largely in American hands. Seemingly unfriendly gestures
are being made by the autonomous Canadian Radio-Tele-

vision and Telecommunications Commission to strip the cable TV commercials coming into Canada from U.S. border stations in order to provide a financial base for Canadian programming. The membership of "Canadian unions" is becoming much more restless under American control, and rapid moves toward autonomy are taking place among the teamsters, construction workers, railway workers and chemical workers.

Some other faint thunder is heard here and there in different parts of Canada, but does that really mean lightning is about to follow? Is the age of Canadian immobilism and benign somnolence coming to an end? Canadian nationalists might indeed wish this were so, but their aspirations are as premature as the darker American suspicions.

Everyone was looking for a toehold on the problem, . . . but none was immediately apparent. . . . Perhaps the answer . . . lay somewhere in the deeper recesses of the elusive Canadian psyche. Some sort of shifting internal deadlock in Canada suggested itself, but how could it ever be uncovered? It may take an unconventional imagination to probe the dynamics of Canadian-American relations at present. As with the ice floes of the Canadian north, the greater preponderance lies beneath the surface. My aim here is not to explore the merits of the immediate issues, nor to air the grievances on either side, but to probe the difficult substratum where the problems have their source. What is developing now is rooted in those antecedent dramas of history and those formative casts of mind that push periodically to center stage. To quote one of our better known Canadian poets and balladeers, Leonard Cohen, "let us compare mythologies."

A Look Backward

In the year of the American Bicentennial, retrospective reflections are the order of the day. Among the most compelling is the work of the American historian Louis Hartz who, in *The Founding of New Societies,* explained how countries of the New World grew and developed within the matrix of that set of beliefs that existed at the moment of their birth. The "fragment" of the Old World that was planted in new soil was a seed carrying John Locke's philosophy of liberalism and freedom. "Born free," Americans must be allowed to become equal. The inner drive has a compelling hold, and, Hartz suggests, "cannot tolerate an accommodation of degree."

Much that was later to emerge as the ideology of American bourgeois society had its roots in that *forma mentis* or the pristine cast of mind of this liberalism. As U.S. history evolved, through Jacksonian democracy, the New Deal, and the Great Society, Hartz maintains that this ethos became "a moral absolute, a national essence, a veritable way of racial life." This ideological leaven pervaded the search for the solution to ills such as the problem of blacks and poverty.

The very dogma that produced the ferocity of the American Civil War was reiterated in the moral brinkmanship of the cold war. The American liberal ethos, in Hartz' interpretation, proclaims that "the world is really one," and this ideology provides Americans "with a shield against the Saracen [and] the only imaginable moral way of dealing with the man outside the West."

A distinct economic ideology formed an integral part of American liberalism. Free exchange, freely arrived at, always and inherently evenhanded, became the filter through which economic life was viewed. If economic practice did not live up to this prescription, the function of national policy was to restructure the environment to appear to conform to the ideology, from fair trade practices to regulatory agencies and antitrust legislation.

In the 1960s—the coming of age of the multinational corporation—American economic liberalism acquired cosmic wings once more as the economic and moral elements fused. For Roy Ash, the former head of Litton Industries, the world corporation represented a "transcendental unity," for "nothing can stop an idea whose time has come." This global vision pervades the American view of much of what has transpired in Canada. Canadian concerns with the integrity of the nation-state, or the preservation of political and cultural autonomy, receive short shrift against this symphonic resonance of global progress ringing in American ears. Fair dealing, the justice inherent in the marketplace, the sanctity of contracts that have been freely entered into by both parties—these serve as a moral shield against the seemingly outmoded objections that Canadians raise. Such an attitude deeply imbues the outlook of American officialdom as well as American business. The U.S. State Department, while sharing the traditional but limited American skepticism about its own corporations, takes a stand on opposing any Canadian legislation that appears to be either retroactive or discriminatory against American interests.

Thus Americans hold firmly to the implicit premise that all that has transpired to date in Canadian-American relations has, by and large, been evenhanded and mutually beneficial. There have, admittedly, been marginal problems in this vast web of interconnections, but a strong tradition of open lines of communication and administrative flexibility has been, and will be, able to resolve the difficulties.

The cumulative political effect with which we now have to contend in Canada appears as the result of unintended and unforeseen consequences; blind spots were at least as operative on the Canadian as on the American side. But the liberal ethos now provides the moral basis for downgrading and tuning out the difficult, unwieldy, and ultimately dangerous problem of the vast American presence. Those who uphold the code of square dealing and who expect their partners to do the same find that the frail Canadian nationalist rhetoric seems to saddle them with a bad conscience. But they tend to reassure themselves that they have played by the rules of the game and the rules carry no particular compensatory provisions for losers ("handicaps," in rare cases, must be specified at the outset). How, in any case, can there be "losers" in a game whose rules are always "even-steven"? When some understanding is forthcoming, it tends at the same time to echo Lyndon Johnson's first public reference to the Canadian-American relationship: "Canada is such a close neighbor and such a good neighbor that we always have plenty of problems there. They are kind of like problems in the hometown."

The latest expressions of American policy bear clearer marks of recognition of the Canadian situation, but are still not easily budged from the traditional stance. Richard Vine, a deputy assistant secretary in the U.S. State Department, went over the ground recently before the House of Representatives Subcommittee on International Political and Military Affairs. While sympathizing with the "Canadian effort to promote expanded economic and cultural autonomy," he recognized the problems involved: "National controls can rarely be expanded without some impact, usually adverse, on established interests in the area of control. . . . The U.S. government has a responsibility to protect the American interests affected to the extent possible and appropriate."

Friendly personal relations, extensive consultation and administrative flexibility are desirable in themselves, but serve to disguise, even from Americans, the hidden rigidity of American policy. The friendly tone still continues with talk of "interdependence" and "mutual benefits" but it is entirely geared to the dubious objective of the preservation of the status quo. For Americans to insist on nondiscrimination in Canadian policies is tantamount to suggesting that we continue to play blindman's buff with the overwhelming American presence. For Americans to continue to insist on nonretroactive policies only is to abort from the outset any possibility of fundamental change. Together, the two pillars of U.S. State Department policy seem to some Canadians merely a license for cosmetic changes. . . .

But on the other side, the unpreparedness is just as great. Many Canadians greeted Nixon's declaration of the end of "the special relationship" with an inaudible but vast sigh of relief. But they were nevertheless still hard put to answer concretely and in some detail the increasingly truculent question, "What do Canadians want?"

The Role of Liberalism

I'm struck by the clarity of the American sense of history: in the beginning, the Americans created America. And ever since, they've been consulting their beginning, the way fundamentalists consult the book of Genesis. . . . Canadians don't have such a clear sense of when things began and ended.—*Northrop Frye* [Canadian critic]

What appears to many as the paralyzing deadlock of Canadian policy toward the United States, the substantial acquiescence by Canadians in their own takeover, stems from the effects of two different systems of belief that remain out of phase: Canadian liberalism, the credo of the dominant elite culture in Canada, and Canadian populism that grows out of a "homestead mentality." While elements of both systems may be present in the same individuals and in the same political parties and while we must ride roughshod over the fine points and exceptions, these two casts of mind are, so to speak, the two psychic horns of the English-speaking Canadian dilemma.

Canadian liberalism is a close cousin of the American variety. Their origins are common but the cadences and mode of development in Canada differ. The ingesting of nineteenth-century British liberalism was the inevitable consequence of the pride Canadians initially took in their colonial status. Philosophy, economics, politics and law had Oxbridge and Westminster as their respective models. Rhodes scholars and other cadres of the able and affluent went to England for many generations to pay homage to civilization at its apogee. They returned to slip into the waiting positions in business, finance, the universities and the civil service. The global perspectives of nineteenth-century England became the official Canadian credo. Free trade (at least in theory if not in practice) and free markets, civil liberties and parliamentary government, would bring the latter-day millennium of the Enlightenment—English style. Oxford accents sometimes sat uneasily atop Canadian French and barely masked a native Ottawa Valley shrewdness, but the prerogatives of shouldering manfully the delegated responsibilities of the Empire were the order of the day.

The loosening of ties with Britain in the interwar period had no more dramatic consequences for national self-consciousness than that of a dutiful and dependent adolescent reluctantly leaving home at last. The country's self-image never rose in stature above Mackenzie King's truculent ambivalence toward Britain and his seemingly cunning flirtation with the United States. [Prime Minister William Lyon] Mackenzie King stated to the American minister in Ottawa in 1935 that Canada was prepared to loosen its British ties and take "the American road," if a good trade agreement with the United States could be arranged.

The trade agreements were eventually forthcoming for reasons of their own, and the Second World War, in turn, brought a more substantial entente and integration between the two countries under King's direction. King became a good deal more suspicious of "the American road" toward the end of his life, but he had set a pattern followed in broad outline by successive Canadian prime ministers.

[Former Prime Minister] Lester Pearson's views heralded a transformation in Canadian opinion to "internationalism," leapfrogging the rather suspect and parochial elements of nationalism. This shining aura overlay the close ties being knotted together under the pressures of the cold war, the joint continental defense agreements, and the open-door policy to all things American. Few paused to wonder at the rather limited range of the "internationalism" we were, in fact, practicing.

Among the most important new influences was the rise of mass education in the postwar period and the redirection of large numbers of Canadian university students from graduate study in Great Britain to the United States. The intellectual atmosphere and assumptions of the University of Chicago, MIT, Harvard and Columbia became the norms of expanding Canadian university staffs and of middle-rank and key civil servants.

In the area of economics, the drums began to beat once more for free trade, and by close analogy for free capital movement. When the institutional form of this capital increasingly became the highly visible hand of the multinational corporation, Canadian economists regilded this new phenomenon with the old paint of Adam Smith. Nothing really new was happening, they maintained, and a carte blanche welcome was to be the policy of the postwar decades. Whatever second thoughts arose in Ottawa were soon suppressed under the old mercantile wisdom of not looking gift horses in the mouth and genuine fears of unemployment. Political time-horizons were short and long-term consequences would look after themselves.

Among the more euphoric prophets of the liberal ethos, elegiac notions arose of Canada as an "international nation," bypassing all that embarrassing, chauvinistic talk of nationhood, which, as everyone knew, simply led to wars. (Whom would Canada attack?) This sentimental miasma produced a comprehensive integrated vision that legitimized the American tide—a vision liberal to its core. In brief summary its components were as follows: an international community seemingly without its constituent component— nations; national intellectual "excellence" without the parochialism" of national traditions, a community of scholars without any special concern for those indigenous boundaries which shape the direction of national inquiry (the inquiry that *produces* knowledge rather than simply living off everyone else's insights); an economy without specificity—manufactured goods as well as resources are all "commodities," faceless units of exchange in both the domestic and international economy. As the gold rush developed for Canadian resources, the door was opened wider still by the conventional economic wisdom. It maintained that there can, by definition, be no overdevelopment in any sector, if "comparative advantage" is pursued under the aegis of the "market."

The Economic Council of Canada, the government's official advisory body, was under the full sway of this economic wisdom. It never deemed the problem of foreign investment in Canada worthy of a full and proper study, even though hundreds of other topics were closely scrutinized. The debate on foreign investment was launched instead by a tiny subculture of economists and politicians who refused to take liberal rhetoric and neoclassical economic theory at face value. The chief documents to emerge were the Gordon Commission Report (1958), the Watkins Report (1968), the Wahn Report (1970) and the Gray Report (1972). They all tried to deal with the issues of Canadian independence in various ways that straddled economics and politics. A picture began to emerge of the "truncation" of Canadian industry—branch plants devoid of research and development facilities, dependent on marketing and purchasing decisions centralized in U.S. head offices—and an overdeveloped resource sector that provided relatively less employment than equivalent manufacturing activity.

The picture was of course mixed, for foreign capital did provide increased employment, paid taxes, and brought new technological and management techniques into the country. But foreign investment was clearly not foreign aid. The specific balance-of-payments effects of foreign investment were difficult to isolate, but one study may give a very rough indication of the magnitudes involved in the two-way flow. The short-term and long-term inflow of capital to Canada between 1950 and 1974 was around $20 billion. This was matched by an outflow of slightly over $40 billion in the same period ($7 billion interest payments, $17 billion in dividends and $16 billion in "service charges," such as license and management fees).

The Science Council of Canada began to fill in the picture where the Economic Council feared to tread. Its 1972 study, *Innovation and the Structure of Canadian Industry,* by Pierre L. Bourgault, noted:

> We are the world's largest producer of nickel, but we are net importers of stainless steel and manufactured nickel products, including "cold climate" nickel-cadmium batteries; we are the world's second largest producer of aluminum, but we import it in its more sophisticated forms. . . . We are the world's largest exporter of pulp and paper, but we import much of our fine paper and virtually all of the highly sophisticated paper, such as backing for photographic film and dielectric papers for use in electronic components; we are one of the world's principal sources of platinum, but it is all exported for refining and processing and reimported in finished forms; we are large exporters of natural gas and petroleum, but we are net importers of petrochemicals; and, although we are the world's foremost exporter of raw asbestos fibres, we are net importers of manufactured asbestos products.

For a country with a higher than average unemployment problem, the low employment content of these resource exports should have meant something. The issue has now been recognized, but the inhibition on effective policy continues despite much talk in recent years about an "industrial strategy" to increase the manufacturing content of our exports.

Nothing was more emblematic of the whole mood of resignation to the incoming tide than the inability of the External Affairs Department to deal with the issue of the extension of American law to American subsidiaries located in Canada. Under the Foreign Assets Control Regulations (the Trading with the Enemy Act), the Sherman Act and Section 7 of the Clayton Act, the American government retains the primary jurisdiction in deciding which countries its foreign subsidiaries can or cannot trade with, when they might or might not discuss mergers, and so on. The divergence from Canadian policy in these matters was often marked, particularly in regard to the American embargo on trade with China, and up until very recently in regard to trade with Cuba.

The crux of the issue, however, lies neither in the value

of potential exports to communist countries which have been forgone, nor in whether American antitrust law has had "good" or "bad" effects on the Canadian industrial structure. There may be legitimate debate about both these points, but the central question is the intrusion of American jurisdiction into a great segment of the Canadian economy through the insistence on the control of U.S. subsidiaries. An elaborate administrative apparatus encompassing several U.S. government departments is set up to try to ensure effective compliance with U.S. foreign economic policy and to impose severe penalties in case of violation. There are no "problems," of course, as long as the foreign economic policies of the two countries are congruent.

The records of the Joint Ministerial Committees of the two countries reveal much symbolic table-pounding, but the Canadians never produced a single workable proposal to implement Canadian sovereignty. The Americans, in turn, never budged an inch in principle, although they were prepared to grant case-by-case exemptions under Washington's total discretion.

Arnold Heeney was the top Canadian diplomat of the period and a living embodiment of the liberal vision. Along with the senior American diplomat Livingston Merchant, he produced the 1965 report entitled *Principles of Partnership,* which put forward the proposal that problems between the two countries be settled discreetly in the diplomatic corridors before they erupted as "public positions." But the report did contain the single blanket proposal that American extraterritorial law operating in Canada be unilaterally revoked by the United States. Paragraph 61 stated: "We strongly recommend that the two governments examine promptly the means, through issuance by the United States of a general license or adoption of other appropriate measures, by which this irritant may be removed. . . ."

I was involved in a governmental task force at the time, studying the broad range of issues relating to foreign investment in Canada and was intrigued by the origins and

fate of this proposal. In a July 1967 interview with Mr.
Heeney, he expressed some belated uneasiness about the
onrushing economic integration of Canada and the United
States. But he confessed, somewhat shamefacedly, that the
one original proposal of the report had come, to his own
surprise, from Livingston Merchant, his American counterpart. He had not himself seen at any time how the problem
could be solved.

I discovered later that the proposal had been blocked by
the U.S. Treasury Department and never got anywhere. But
the interview summed up for me the limits of Ottawa's
liberal vision: the lurking regret and unwitting day-to-day
participation in knotting together and smoothing out the
strands of Canadian dependence; the excellence in soft-shoe
tactics and the haplessness in strategy. After 1968, when
legal proposals began to emerge for the first time from both
the Watkins and Wahn reports that showed how American
extraterritorial jurisdiction could be effectively blocked by
firm action in Canada, the Canadian government ran true
to form by deciding that the political costs of marring the
American relationship in this way were too high. Nothing
was done. In retrospect, it appears to have been an era of
flatulent rhetoric and faceless floundering best exhibited by
the two ministers of external affairs, Paul Martin and
Mitchell Sharp.

While it may appear dubious to root concrete and massive economic and political dilemmas in Canada in the
astigmatism of liberal theory, exactly that cast of mind, I
believe, is the key to Canada's "silent surrender." Canadian
liberalism was all of a piece: a sentimental internationalism,
a pussyfooting "quiet diplomacy," and a procrustean view
of multinational corporations as ever-friendly "market"
phenomena.

As it happened, liberalism proclaimed, and indeed celebrated, the nation's nonexistence. Society was reduced by
definition to a collection of self-seeking individuals; the
state was merely the instrument of the protection of property

and the enforcement of contract. The concept of the nation as such entered obtrusively only in awkward and negative ways: in its economic incarnation it was the progenitor of tariffs and other restrictions on the "natural" free flow of trade and capital. Such a natural flow would make, as everyone from Adam Smith to [economist] Milton Friedman knew, for grand global harmony.

The absence of a distinct and traumatic moment of self-creation in Canada gave great power and longevity to an imported British liberalism and its subsequent American version, despite the vital threat it posed to Canada's inner integrity as a nation. Missing as always from such colonial projection was the internally rooted sense of a national self, that is, an independent political culture with its accompanying symbols to evoke and protect Canadian nationhood.

What was thereby so effectively blotted out was the problem of power, particularly the locus of economic power. Thus when power began to shift out of the Canadian economy to Chicago, New York and Washington by virtue of the highly visible and active hand of the multinational corporation, and by virtue of our dependence on Washington's legal and economic policies, we were barely conscious that anything of importance had happened. All we could ask was whether the "market" was functioning properly and whether profits (somewhere, anywhere) were being "maximized."

But the nemesis of the twentieth century must come sooner or later to the adherents of nineteenth-century credos. So, too, this era moved to its grand moment of culmination when one event lit up the entire Canadian reality. On December 6, 1971, Prime Minister [Pierre Elliott] Trudeau visited President Nixon in Washington on a strange quest. He emerged from this meeting elated and euphoric, for the American President had granted Canada something quite "fantastic." Nothing less than a Canadian Declaration of Independence had emerged out of Washington. Presumably that is where it now had to be sought. However demeaning to Canadian sensibilities, a high degree of political realism was involved in this backhanded recognition of how far American control had extended. As Trudeau put the matter the following day to the Canadian Parliament: "He [the President] assured me that it was in the clear interests of the United States to have a Canadian neighbour, not only independent both politically and economically but also one which was confident that the decisions and policies in each of these sectors would be taken by Canadians in their own interests, in defence of their own values, and in pursuit of their own goals." *Noblesse oblige.* The event was "fantastic" in more ways than one: for Canadian liberalism, the head office is always elsewhere.

The Role of Populism

But there is a backstage protagonist that has only sporadically appeared on the stage of Canadian-American relations. That protagonist is not, in the first instance, Canadian nationalism, but a more diffuse, unfocused and potentially very powerful force in Canadian politics—grass-roots populism. Its essential cast of mind is the homestead mentality and its articulation is through the politics of space.

In the inner recesses of the Canadian self-image there remains the indelible imprint of the pioneer struggle with the land—the vanquishing of hostile forest, stubborn rock and parched prairie. There is the lasting trauma of outliving bleak winters into a late spring, of existing on the precarious margin of a short Canadian agricultural season. This is the psychic crucible in which Canadian populism was shaped—in latent anxiety, in wariness and reticence and in a sense of ongoing silent siege.

But turning no-man's-land into one's own homestead carries with it ingrained or natural rights that accrue to the survivor. A political sense of earned jurisdiction over a vanquished space that was, at least in principle, inviolable and sacrosanct, became the nuclear element of political identity that arose in the Canadian psyche. Economic and political jurisdiction on the homestead should be untrammeled, and any trespass or political infringement would be resisted.

In the Canadian consciousness, as in Canadian history, the homestead precedes the establishment of the state. This mental landscape that harks back to the primal (even if recent) origins of the country provides the political footing from which the state itself in its various roles may be either substantially endorsed or roundly opposed. The specific political characteristics of the homestead mentality were, often enough, vague; without a strong ideological base and essentially anti-establishment in its orientation, it remained tied by a powerful navel cord to the land either in fact or in persistent imagination. The essential political framework was space rather than class.

Canadian populism is not unique but seems more firmly entrenched than American populism and more readily articulated in a federal system, particularly as the distance from Ottawa increases. Among its distinct features is the very high priority given to preserving social order over established territory. The national symbol in Canada is not the cowboy or the covered wagon—those self-reliant symbols of rough justice individually dispensed—but the opposite, the "Mountie," the lone representative and guarantor of central authority in barely policed areas who "always gets his man." Canadians are prepared to support a virtually unlimited role of the state in the preservation of social order and in the concomitant assertion of sovereignty over the "homestead writ large," the "Dominion from sea to sea." The evidence for such a deep-seated but widely pervasive cast of mind is necessarily impressionistic and scattered, only surfacing occasionally.

The primary concern is with the land. Thus it happened that from the apparently least nationalist part of the country, the Maritime Provinces [Nova Scotia, New Brunswick, and Prince Edward Island], there emerged the most stringent legislation barring foreigners from owning land. This has been repeated in Saskatchewan, and has now become an active concern in virtually all provinces, and the federal government is prepared to follow their lead. On September 5, 1975, Prime Minister Trudeau sent a letter to the ten provincial premiers offering to introduce federal legislation granting the provinces the right to restrict foreign ownership of property.

The priority given to land, and the corresponding lethargy regarding industry and technology in the Canadian imagination, were never more dramatically illustrated than in an incident which occurred in 1969. At that time the Humble Oil Company, seeking a Northwest Passage to export Alaskan oil by ship, sent the American vessel *Manhattan* through the Arctic waters. This raised the specter of whether Canadian sovereignty in Arctic waters was being challenged or jeopardized (the legal issues of which we must bypass here). Recall that this was prior to the oil and gas boom in the Canadian north, so that what was at issue was the fate of the ice floes and glaciers in a virtually uninhabited part of the country. Suddenly, Canadian newspapers from coast to coast, most of which had traditionally welcomed the takeover of Canadian businesses, now wrote as many as two or three editorials a day in great alarm. "Fly the Canadian Flag" read the hysterical headline of the now-defunct *Toronto Telegram*, a newspaper that had viewed with complacency the passing of 70 percent of southern Ontario's industry to American control.

But this same consciousness underlies (quite apart from the economic issues) Canada's perennial concern with fishing zones, and more recently the 200-mile offshore limit, and its substantial initiative at the Conference on the Law of the Sea. It is also the homestead mentality that may account for the otherwise totally inexplicable Canadian preoccupation with water. Canada possesses something on the order of 20 to 50 percent of the world's supply of fresh water, and an enormous amount runs off annually into the sea, perhaps 6 percent of the world's runoff. (As usual, we have no exact statistics.) Yet one of the silent but absolute premises that

unites Canadians from coast to coast is that not a single drop
should be exported, no matter how great the surplus supply
may be. As the former premier of British Columbia, W. A.
C. Bennett, who had never hesitated to sell anything to the
highest bidder, once stated: "Even to talk about selling water
is ridiculous. Water is our heritage and you don't sell your
heritage."

Without wishing in any way here to advocate the export
of water, or to minimize the enormous environmental issues
involved, it seems clear from the data we do have that the potential export of a fraction of our surplus water might easily
exceed in value any single item of Canadian exports. It is
now completely wasted. My purpose, however, is to indicate
one of the areas where the deep-seated homestead mentality
has surfaced in the political arena and has held fast. The
issue of water is as "self-evident" to Canadians at large, as
it is puzzling to everyone else.

Land and water are the clues to the underlying attitudes
in the new phase of Canadian nationalism which centers on
resources, particularly energy resources. The important question in Canada is the extent to which the same cast of mind
is now beginning to surface on these closely related issues.
As the leading Canadian historian, Donald Creighton, a
man of conservative bent, explained in 1970:

Canadians instinctively regard their natural resources in a very
special light. . . . These natural resources are not looked upon as
ordinary assets—things the Canadians have built or acquired themselves. They are regarded as part of the original endowment of
nature, as the birthright of Canada. Many of them are not owned
absolutely, as they would be in the United States, by private enterprises. They are properties in which the Crown retains a right,
which it has sometimes converted into public ownership, for the
beneficial interest of the people of Canada.

It appears that public opinion supports this position. A
Gallup Poll of May 16, 1973, asked whether the "Canadian
government should nationalize our energy resources, such
as oil and gas." Of Canadians across the country 48 percent
replied in the affirmative, while 36 percent were opposed. . . .
A similar Gallup Poll taken in the first week of November

1975 indicated a figure of 51 percent in favor of nationalizing oil and gas and 31 percent opposed.

Thus it would be a mistake to interpret the renewed call for reclaiming our oil and gas, as well as other resources such as potash, as a sudden spread of socialist ideology. The activation of the federal government's corporation, Petro-Canada, as well as similar corporations in provinces such as Alberta, Newfoundland and Saskatchewan reflect an extension of this territorial ethic, not radical in its complexion but essentially conservative. It was a Conservative government that nationalized electricity in Ontario in 1910 and Conservative governments now operate in Alberta and Newfoundland while a social democratic government operates in Saskatchewan.

Thus, populist politics in Canada are indeed the politics of space. Canadian sensitivity to the extraterritorial extension of American law, referred to earlier, has been the chief basis for much unease over American investment. The traditional concern with the integrity of Canadian authority on the "homestead writ large" has far outweighed other considerations such as an unbalanced or truncated economic structure, overdependence on resource development for the U.S. market and a rapidly eroding technological capability.

But the politics of space does not make for a uniform endorsement of state intervention. An indirect legacy of this same cast of mind reinforces the existing struggle of both business and labor against various measures proposed by the federal government. The businessman who struggled to carve out his enterprise "against great odds" will barely tolerate any interference in his prerogative; hence the remarkable campaign mounted by the business community a few years ago against . . . tax reform proposals . . . to fundamentally restructure the business "homestead." Economics was not at issue here (despite much rhetoric about free enterprise) but rather politics, the claim to untrammeled autonomy and jurisdiction of the institutional homestead.

Union leaders who carved out their "homestead," i.e., their union jurisdiction, in the difficult days of the early 1930s, will not tolerate limits on the collective bargaining process—their rightfully earned area of "total authority." In the debate over the government's anti-inflation program of wage and price controls, Canadian labor unions were militantly opposed as were unions in other countries. But a hidden dimension added a particular acrimony to this debate in Canada. Canadian unions were prepared to sink the whole anti-inflation program because it was an intrusion into their political space.

These are not primary but background features of the domestic political scene, and by no means unique to Canada. But in a federal state such as Canada, populism has held on longer and more forcefully, sheltered by the significant provincial enclaves of power. The implicit political game in Canada is somehow to tap this very powerful and widespread populist undercurrent. If successfully achieved on rare occasions, the political payoff can be enormous. This largely accounts, in my view, for the landslide Conservative victories by John Diefenbaker in 1958–59. Diefenbaker appeared as the living image of old-fashioned prairie populism. It also accounts, for quite different reasons—largely because of an image of popular irreverence and iconoclasm—for the substantial Liberal victory of Pierre Trudeau in 1968: the upper-class man in populist clothing.

Populists feel safest when they can have it both ways. While they retain a healthy skepticism of the liberal establishment—the moneyed, the educated and the bureaucracy —they are not prepared to trust their own leaders to govern except on rare occasions. (This syndrome is not unlike that of the British Labour Party's tendency to select its leaders from the graduates of the public school and from Oxbridge.) Populism is more often successful on the provincial rather than the federal scene where the risks of bungling by those without "class" or "experience" are less. In day-to-day politics, populism stands aside as a suspicious but vigilant monitor of potential state intrusions into the equivalent of the homestead, and as a militant guardian of social order and national sovereignty.

Thus at the time of the [1973] OPEC [Organization of Petroleum Exporting Countries] oil embargo, when Americans heard the crisp statements of Canadian intentions not to pool energy shortages with the United States, but instead to cut back on energy exports, they might have discerned several different notes in the chord. First, there was the reaction to the fiasco around the nonexistent reserves centered on the oil companies' misleading figures. Second, the underlying populist sentiment in Canada had now begun to come forward as an ongoing and overt political factor around the resources question. Third, the nationalist message itself had begun to penetrate the political process.

The linking of these latter two elements may be decisive and may become the dominant factor in future Canadian-American relations.

Toward Economic Autonomy

I have overdrawn somewhat the characteristics of the two major casts of mind in Canada. Their elements are often to be found in some combination within the same individual and within . . . [the] major political parties. How do they each relate to the new nationalism?

Modern Canadian nationalism is a relative latecomer to the political scene, barely two decades old. It cannot be understood as a movement, but as a countermovement to the astigmatism of the liberal position. Its aim is to protect the fabric of Canadian society against the autonomous and relentless forces running "free" in the North American market economy.

In their public image in Canada, nationalists stand in some awkward middle position between liberals and populists, somewhat suspect to both sides. Populists tend to regard nationalism as an elite heresy, the inverse image of the liberal ethic in which they have no direct stake, and have therefore largely stood aloof from a full nationalist program. Liberals, in turn, have tended to regard the nationalist position as a retrogressive, inward-looking throwback, vaguely populist, for which there is no clear place in the modern world.

Nevertheless, despite these suspicions, and because of the palpable force of circumstances, a limited form of nationalism has quietly spread to a wide segment of the population and has in its own way outrun the actual membership of nationalist organizations such as the Committee for an Independent Canada.

But there are no optimistic forecasts to be made any more for the recapturing by Canadians of their own economic and cultural autonomy—even though in the modern world, the issue can at best be only a matter of degree. Sometimes it seems to Canadian nationalists, from past experience, that if things can possibly go wrong, they will. Nevertheless, there are solid indications that the major battle in Canada has now begun over the question of resources. Here the populist consciousness may well become fully engaged in the reclaiming of the "homestead" along with nationalists whose concern has traditionally been the wider link between resources and industry. Liberals, in turn, now have cause to see all about them, late in the day as it is, the consequences of their beneficent sleepwalking and defer in a limited way to moderate nationalist arguments.

But none of this in itself necessarily makes for substantial policy changes in Canada. Change, rather, is being galvanized by economic factors: increases in heating and gasoline bills, the vast capital sums that will be needed for pipelines from the north and their attendant inflationary effects, and the major balance-of-payments problems that Canada may anticipate from mounting oil imports.

The nationalist program on energy exports now begins to make sense to many Canadians for it calls for a substantial further reduction in energy exports to the United States. While there is no unanimity on how much or how quickly, a further cut from the 1976 level of 460,000 barrels of oil a day would seem to be warranted, i.e., a more rapid implementation of existing policy.

In regard to natural gas, the Canadian government is following a standpat position, hoping to fulfill existing contracts with the United States—however fraudulent the information on which the 1970 export decision was based—and to meet the domestic shortage with a vastly expensive pipeline from the far north. Since Canadian discoveries of gas in the north are still inadequate to finance a pipeline (3.5 to 5 trillion cubic feet), the intention is to have the pipeline carry jointly Canadian and Alaskan gas, the latter destined for the United States. Total long-term contracts call for the export of 14 trillion cubic feet of Canadian gas to the United States between 1974 and 1995. It is the commitment to these export contracts and the uncertainty about the rate of new discoveries in Alberta and their deliverability that prompts this pipeline policy. Meanwhile, the most easily accessible, high-pressure gas fields (Waterton B.H.K. and Kaybob South) are now under contract to California by the American-owned Alberta and Southern Gas Co. Approximately one trillion cubic feet of gas is exported annually from western Canada, equal to two-thirds of domestic Canadian consumption.

Most nationalists in Canada would argue for a drastic change in government policy. The Mackenzie Valley pipeline would cost some $10 billion to build. It would have substantial disruptive effects on northern ecology and on the native peoples, and would produce a serious inflationary impact on the Canadian economy. This could all be averted by a moratorium on the project contingent on a drastic reduction of gas exports to the United States.

Under sections 17(2) and 85 of the National Energy Board Act such reduction or elimination of licensed exports is legally possible if domestic supply conditions warrant it. The diversion of, say, 10 trillion cubic feet of gas, earmarked for export, to domestic use would add seven years to Can-

ada's gas supply at 1975 consumption rates and would post-
pone the need for this expensive pipeline. While new discoveries were being sought in Alberta, American buyers
might be given three years' notice of the rescinding of our
export agreements and might then contract for whatever
surplus gas they could discover that would begin to fulfill
their overly sanguine 1970 reserve estimates.

Not to be neglected are the long-term political problems
associated with moving Alaskan gas through a Canadian
pipeline to the United States. The claims of native groups
and environmentalists have hardly begun to be met and we
can anticipate that political opposition in this whole area
may be very great. Given the potential strategic importance
of such a pipeline to the United States, the interests of the
American military and intelligence establishments in the
security of such a pipeline may tighten the American embrace on Canada even further, particularly since American
financing and American gas would be centrally involved in
the project. Canadians are not unmindful of the dangers of
creating a land-based Panama Canal-type situation in their
country. The contemplated pipeline treaty between the two
countries may be reassuring, but cannot dissolve the political
and strategic issues. Thus the pipeline carries with it substantial economic, ecological and political risks for Canada,
risks that are too great, in my view, to warrant fulfillment
of our American contracts. It is a precise case in point where
Canada must, in its own interest, take action that is retroactive and discriminatory.

The populist response to such a program and to the
larger question of a new resource policy is not easily pre-
dictable. Populism is more at home as the unofficial opposition in day-to-day politics, and is more of an impulse than a
movement. Much will depend on the political image the
immediate issue assumes. If it comes up as an issue of social
order *cum* sovereignty, one may expect widespread public
support for greater Canadian control of our natural resources and great pressures on whatever government is in

power. For example, a popular move would be for the government, through Petro-Canada, to buy out one of the major oil companies such as Imperial Oil.

The attempt to deal more forcefully with the high percentages of American control of the manufacturing industry is not on the immediate political agenda. This will have to await a further development of public consciousness around the issue of a national industrial strategy designed to integrate more directly our resource production and manufacturing activity. All that Canadian nationalists can hope for now is that the few cultural initiatives will be sustained, that the screening and review process on foreign companies will be expanded and that resource nationalism will become the political base for expanded initiatives by Canadians to become masters in their own house.

The Central Role of Power

Such is the direction of the Canadian political endowment at the moment when the country is gathering its second wind. Hence the . . . American ambassador to Canada, Thomas O. Enders, may have been somewhat premature in his maiden speech to the Canadian Club of Ottawa last March [1976] when he stated: "We are both conscious that the end of the 'special relationship' frees us both from historical hang-ups in pursuing our interests." In the traditional terms in which the Canadian-American relationship has been conducted, he was perfectly correct.

But a realignment of the old liberal credo, wearing its complementary faces in both countries, may not be the best preparation for what is to come. In Canada, an old set of "historical hang-ups" may just be coming into place. For example, Saskatchewan's intention to acquire half the province's potash capacity (largely American-owned) may be better understood in the light of what we have been discussing. This prospect poses the dilemma that the province would then have control of one-third of the U.S. potash supply. "Although welcome," the ambassador added, "statements that this power would be used benignly are not adequate reassurance."

The power question in all its new and interlocking dimensions goes to the heart of the matter in Canadian-American relations. The ambassador did sympathize in his speech with "the assertion of Canadian national purpose" and did not contest the right of Canadians to expropriate "provided it is paid for fully, promptly, and effectively." But this expanded liberalism does not settle the question of power, and such an underlying and often hidden issue as potash may be the forerunner of similar problems yet to arise.

The power question—and there is none more important —is now on the agenda, and it is clear that the fundamental and long-standing lopsidedness of the distribution of power as it affects Canadian interests needs major correction. Canadians may be forgiven for a sense of *déjà vu*. Statements that American power in Canada, at so many different levels, "would be used benignly" have a remarkably familiar ring and are not, as the ambassador states, "adequate reassurance."

It is on the resolution of this central item on our joint agenda that everything now turns.

WAKING UP FROM THE CANADIAN DREAM [2]

Every Canadian schoolchild for the last 70 years has been brought up to believe the most celebrated of national aphorisms: "The 19th century was the century of the United States. The 20th century belongs to Canada."

That strong assertion was uttered in 1904 by a prime minister, Sir Wilfrid Laurier, and has been repeated in one variation or another by every prime minister since then. In 1971, Pierre Elliott Trudeau referred to Canada as "a land of limitless promise, a land, perhaps, on the threshold of

[2] From "Waking Up from the Canadian Dream," by Gerald Clark, editor of the Montreal *Star*. New York *Times Magazine*. p 40-1+. Je. 6, '76. © 1976 by The New York Times Company. Reprinted by permission.

greatnesss." By 1976 his refrain had altered radically. "Canada," Trudeau told a national television audience, "faces enormous challenges in the years ahead. Our ability to meet these challenges will depend primarily on our willingness to adapt our attitudes and habits to the facts of life."

One of these facts is that Canada's resources are not bottomless wonders—a simple enough judgment, yet it jars the Canadian psyche and self-confidence. Another—and Canadians are now going through the turmoil of discovering it —is that they aren't as eager as their parents were to share the country with a mass of strangers. In the past, immigration filled the wide open spaces—at least the reasonably hospitable strip, a couple of hundred miles wide, that runs alongside the United States border. As recently as the fifties, Canadians were comforted by the notion that the north country could be opened up, and that's where new settlers would go. This was exposed as a myth when it became known that simply to build an ordinary house, worth perhaps $30,000 in a southern region, would cost a minimum of $175,000.

The questions growing, anyway, were these: How big a population did Canadians really desire? With a threat of increased pollution and crime, wouldn't there be merit in keeping the country small and manageable? At least by inference—if not overtly—racism has helped frame the questions.

Canada is still overwhelmingly white; 96 percent of its people are of European descent. But racial tensions have arisen, even when they're disguised as something else—such as overcrowding. In Vancouver, for instance, Mayor Arthur Phillips said that about half the population increase in his city was due to immigration and this created a housing shortage. "Immigrants have brought talent, money and culture," Phillips said, "but they have not brought land." Thus, he concluded, this was primarily a spatial question, not a racial question.

But the men and women who heard him—members of a joint parliamentary committee examining the broad issue of immigration—knew something of the background. Vancouver, because of its moderate climate and top salaries, lures from the East many Canadians who compete for jobs in a time of high unemployment. Tempers become tight, especially since the city also entices—because of its location on the Pacific coast—many Asian and East Indian immigrants. Bands of schoolboys have attacked Pakistanis; Sikh temples have been desecrated. Even without violent antipathy, the mood is reflected by a crop of sick jokes. "I'm starting a collection for a Pakistani family whose house is on fire," says a supposed humorist. "So far I've collected six gallons of gasoline to keep it going."

Changing Views Toward Immigrants

Canadians traditionally have had a kind of missionary zeal, a feeling that they have an obligation to share their wealth with the less well-endowed. This has enabled about four million people, including 300,000 political refugees, to migrate to Canada since the end of the Second World War —a figure that in terms of comparative populations would mean 40 million to the United States. But why, many Canadians are now asking, should this missionary ardor persist?

The question was never raised so forcefully before because the matter of race was not relevant. White Europeans were happy to line up at immigration offices abroad and await visas for the land of opportunity. As late as 1967, almost 80 percent of the immigration flow was from Europe. But then Europe became affluent. Europeans, with improved standards and opportunities of their own, were less inclined to look to Canada. By 1974 they made up only 39 percent of the immigrant force, while Asians had risen from 6 percent to 23 percent. Canadians, who had never before been exposed to the quandary of Birmingham, Alabama, or Birmingham, England, and therefore could not be called racist, now openly say they are apprehensive of blacks from the Caribbean and browns from India and Pakistan.

"Openly" is perhaps the wrong word; the reaction is mostly under the breath, as though the exponent knows it is improper to suggest any curtailment based on color. But the cumulative effect is loud and clear. The parliamentary committee operated for 35 weeks, holding nearly 50 public hearings in 21 cities. Only 25 percent of the briefs from organizations or individuals appearing in person wanted tight or total controls on immigration. The majority said much the same as a Toronto clergyman who expressed a worry that any restrictions would ignore "the principles of social justice and humanitarian concerns."

In contrast, 60 percent of the letter writers, protected by privacy, wanted a stop to all immigration or all nonwhite immigration. The committee was obliged to note in its report to Parliament: "A fear of rapid increase in the numbers of nonwhites from the third world was the most prevalent sentiment in individual letters, and many cited racial tension and conflict, or at best erosion of the Canadian identity."

By United States criteria, there are no black ghettos in Canada. The closest resemblance to a ghetto—Africville, a shantytown in Halifax, Nova Scotia, whose first inhabitants traced their ancestry to slaves brought north by loyalists after the American Revolution—was torn down in 1966. For blacks, who make up less than 1 percent of the population. ghettoization is no different from what it is for Greeks or Portuguese or Italians—an economic rather than a racial limitation of Canadian life.

Overt discrimination is relatively slight. In Montreal, civil-liberties investigators find that of every 10 complaints of restrictions encountered by blacks when they are seeking housing, only three have any foundation. "We take the view," said a black social worker, "that since the figure is so small it is better to walk around the corner and look for other accommodations rather than raise a fuss." Crime is not an issue; the statistics for black victims or perpetrators are about the same as for whites.

Much of this impressive record resolves around a less impressive factor: an immigration selection procedure that has never been fully altruistic. Of the 200,000 blacks in Canada, between 60 and 70 percent have arrived only in the last decade, and while some are political refugees from Haiti or draft evaders from the United States, the bulk have been admitted on the strength of superior education and skills. These nurses, teachers and scientific technicians—mostly from Jamaica, Trinidad and other Caribbean islands—find good jobs and enter the mainstream.

US Immigrants to Canada

Britain, until 1971, was the biggest single source of immigrants to Canada. But that year for the first time the United States took the lead, with 24,366 Americans moving [there]. . . . This continued through 1972, and although the United Kingdom regained the lead in 1973, the number of American immigrants rose to 25,242. (In contrast, only 8,951 Canadians left for the United States, underscoring the fact that the old brain drain, which for generations had afflicted Canada, was reversed.) The peak of American immigration was reached in 1974, with 26,541 coming to Canada. Then the trend faltered . . . [with] an inflow of only 16,225 for the first nine months of 1975.

Changes in Canadian immigration regulations may have contributed to the decline . . . [in 1975], but the overall pattern appears to be related to conditions of life in the United States. The unpopularity of the Vietnam war obviously drove out some people—apart from draft evaders, many academics chose Canada—while others were attracted by work opportunities and relative serenity on the streets. But the termination of the war ended part of the motivation, while a decline in Canadian college enrollments—and an increase in Canadian Ph.D.'s looking for appointments—spoiled the chances for American academics.

How well do Americans integrate in Canadian life? They do not congregate in any kind of immigrant ghettos; they're absorbed immediately in the general community. Acceptance and adjustment come easily. Language, currency, customs and values present few surprises; Americans watch the same television programs they enjoyed at home and follow the primaries in newspapers that look familiar in format. There is little pressure on an American immigrant to make a conscious effort to become a Canadian. A survey . . . [in 1974] by Ottawa's citizenship branch showed that Americans were slow in taking out Canadian citizenship (for which five years' residence is required). Many, after 10 years or more . . . , still cling to United States citizenship. But lately, to judge from letters received by the citizenship branch, there has been a tendency for Americans to request Canadian papers when eligible—for business reasons or to qualify for jobs in teaching or the civil service, or out of personal conviction. In general, younger immigrants are less hesitant than their elders to switch allegiance.

What Future Immigration Policy?

What of the future? What kind of immigration should Canada permit? What kind of country does it want to be? These were questions with which the parliamentary committee occupied itself in evaluating the public debate and taking into account a Green Paper on immigration, an official document that offered a variety of options without committing the Government to any of them. The Green Paper had already observed that after a spectacular increase in fertility, which reached a peak in 1957, the birth rate today stands at only 1.8 per woman. At this pace, Canada will attain a population of only about 26 million (from the present 22.5 million) by the year 2001 without immigration. With immigration, however, the Green Paper suggested the target could range realistically between 28.4 million and 34.6 million, depending on the needs of the Canadian economy and labor market.

The committee, made up of eight Senators and 15 members of the House of Commons, came to the conlusion that the answer for Canada is not in an "open-door" policy. It called for "a policy of moderation"—a partly closed door—to maintain a population level of 28 million during the first half of the 21st century (not simply the year 2001). Thus, Canada, it said, should welcome a minimum of 100,000 immigrants a year (compared with a total of 218,000 in 1974).

The committee was divided on whether to suggest an upper limit, such as prevails in the United States (290,000 a year since 1965), and it compromised by saying the Government, when formulating a target for each year, should not treat the figure of 100,000 as a maximum as well as minimum. It also said that since Canada's capacity to attract Europeans had diminished and the country must look to other parts of the world, there should be no discrimination "on the basis of race, creed, nationality, ethnic origin and sex."

Lofty and well-intentioned as those words are—and individual members of the committee emphasize their commitment to them—the fact is that the large majority of newcomers in the future automatically will be Europeans. The reduced target figure will compensate for the decline in number of applicants from Europe, and the point system —based on a person's education and work skills—will continue to favor them. Ben Wicks, a syndicated cartoonist, portrays a Canadian immigration officer testing applicants by giving an Englishman and an Italian the easy names of Canadian provinces to spell. Then the officer turns to a colored man and says, "Spell Saskatchewan."

Although the committee said immigrants should not be blamed for urban problems "they have done little to cause," public debate on the issue does not always proceed from that finding. Lord Thomson of Fleet, the Canadian-born newspaper baron, said on a . . . visit to Toronto that the quality of life there has deteriorated. He blamed foreigners —the same Italians, Portuguese, Greeks, Jamaicans and others usually credited with helping to make Toronto one of the most appealing cities on the continent. Lord Thomson did not quote statistics, but opponents of immigration are quick to point to a 37 percent increase in murders in 1975 over 1974. Muggings in the Toronto subway have become sufficiently frequent to require the posting of additional security guards. No one has produced evidence pointing to immigrants as the cause. The official interpretation is probably the logical one: An expanding city inevitably shows some changes in personality. But for advocates of a closed door it is enough to hear this and blame it not on old-time residents but the new ones.

A Testing Time for the Economy

Trudeau today talks of a "New Society," without actually defining what he has in mind, except to say that it should embrace ways to avoid excessive demands on the economy. He exhorts Canadians to drive less and to cut down on the use of electricity—this in a land of untamed wilderness, of roaring rivers, of hydropower just waiting to be tapped! The clichés, alas, are out of date.

Earlier in his administration, Trudeau was preoccupied with Quebec and the dangers of secession; now it is with the economy. What happened in the interval? In broadest terms, Canadians found themselves caught up in a phenomenon they had not encountered before: a combination of high inflation—nearly 11 percent in 1975—and high unemployment, 7.2 percent. The fact that this was a worldwide phenomenon was hardly consoling. Canadians, thanks partly to the encouragement of political soothsayers, had regarded themselves as specially endowed. But three or four years of the inflation-unemployment mixture reduced people's faith in the ability of governments to manage the economy and damaged the assumption that somehow governments would provide answers to unexpected problems—such as the emergence of OPEC [Organization of Petroleum Exporting Countries] and its capacity to undermine industrialized states.

What made this development particularly distressing to Canadians was the shattering of a posture of self-sufficiency in oil. As recently as . . . [1973–1974], they still clung to the lofty forecasts of a 1957 Royal Commission on Canada's economic prospects. So did the Government, in accepting the projection that by 1980 Canadian oil output would be about three million barrels a day.

The figure was seductive, impelling Canadians to believe that not only was there enough oil for their own needs, virtually for ever and ever, but that if they didn't want to be stuck with any excess they'd better unload fast before people abroad discovered other ways of heating their homes or driving their cars. The Trudeau Government, from 1968 to 1972, pursued a prime objective of selling as much oil as possible to the United States; it exerted pressure on Washington to ease its import restrictions, to buy from Alberta oil fields while eastern Canada's needs were filled by tankers from Venezuela.

Then came the [1973 Arab-Israeli] Yom Kippur war and two developments: Ottawa realized that because of the increase in the world price of oil, it would have to cover more of the East's requirements with shipments from Alberta; and the earlier projection of Canada's own capability proved to be vastly exaggerated. Now, having won over the United States as a customer, Canada cut the flow there—from a one-time high of a million barrels a day to 700,000 barrels a day in 1975. It also served notice that this supply will be steadily reduced, ending completely in . . . [1983].

Canada . . . [in 1975] was not even able to satisfy its own demands and became a net importer. As for the projection of three million barrels a day, this has now been reduced to 1,450,000. Since requirements in 1980 will be at least 2,375,000 barrels a day, one does not have to strive hard to recognize that a shortfall of more than 900,000 barrels places Canada in not much more of an enviable position than Holland—that is, at the mercy of OPEC and life generally.

Trudeau Under Fire

On top of that, Canadians were told they were living beyond their means. They had undertaken to give themselves wage increases at a rate roughly twice as high as their American neighbors, despite an economy that was not nearly so productive. This kind of gluttony forced Trudeau ... [in 1975] to introduce wage and price controls, operative until 1978. Later, musing in a television interview, he said, "The economy, the society is out of joint." He questioned the validity of the "free market system" and wondered if "it means there's going to be not less authority in our lives but perhaps more."

The reaction was fierce, and in itself more revealing than Trudeau's own remarks, since, basically, he had been saying much the same for a year or more. But now the president of the biggest labor federation called Trudeau a menace to workers; the president of the biggest bank solemnly warned that if the free enterprise system were to be changed, Trudeau should first call an election. It was a jumpy reflex, indicative of the mood of uncertainty after the surprising imposition of controls, a device Canadians had never been compelled to face in peacetime.

If there was any fault with the television interview, apart from its timing, it was that this was not Prime Minister Trudeau speaking; rather, it was Professor Trudeau thinking aloud, ruminating as he once did in seminars with law students. But his spontaneity caused so much confusion and consternation that a couple of weeks later Trudeau felt constrained to give a formal speech, carefully written in advance, in which he said the same things all over again.

Challenging a "free market system," he said, did not mean an end to private enterprise, which anyway has co-existed a long time with state enterprise—public ownership of power utilities, railways, airlines—and with government control of such items as telephone rates. The question essentially was about the sort of mélange Canada would need in the future, and, in a Galbraithian sense, whether some controls would always be necessary in a modern industrialized society.

Trudeau had no precise answers, and thus only succeeded in creating more doubts about the future. But what he really wanted to do, he made plain, was to start a national debate on where Canada was going, to prepare people to accept some curtailment of old habits that had contributed to an excessive inflation rate. What he didn't say bluntly—but this was implicit—was that in psychological terms, the long-range motive was to reduce *expectations*. No longer, some economists have been saying, should Canadians even hope to repeat the jaunty affluence of the early seventies.

Apart from the controversy over Trudeau's economic stand—a massive march on Ottawa's Parliament Hill attested to labor's anger over wage restraints—there is some disenchantment with him personally. The old Trudeaumania, based on a public's desire for flair in a political leader, has been replaced after eight years by suspicion that Trudeau is too imperious in dealing with his critics and political foes. . . .

Trudeau has shown some awareness that his base may be delicate. The Conservatives have a new national leader, 36-year-old Joe Clark, who, as a member of the House of Commons, stood out, if not for brilliance, at least for tenacity. Trudeau had the measure of Clark's predecessor, Robert Stanfield, and found him easy to handle in debate. Stanfield was a gentleman, disinclined to go for the jugular. Clark, a former newspaperman, is not so inhibited.

In a . . . confrontation with Clark over a highly intense issue in the House of Commons, Trudeau demonstrated remarkable and uncharacteristic self-control. There was none of his old intellectual arrogance. It may have been due to a concern that his public appeal—and that of his Liberal Party—has deteriorated. The . . . [spring 1976] Gallup Poll gives the Conservatives a lead over the Liberals—by 9 points—for the first time in almost a decade.

The Status of Canada's Cities

Canadian cities do not appear to be suffering the hardships of their American counterparts. This country has not experienced the vacating of cities by the middle class, and thus the weakening of the tax base. Moreover, in major centers, such as Montreal and Toronto, the cores have enjoyed a rejuvenation, not only through commercial building but through continuity of attractive housing. Cities . . . do pay a price, in that they are creatures of their provincial governments and often lack the financial autonomy they would like to have. However, this relieves them of the burden faced, for instance, by New York. Most social services, including welfare, are financed at higher levels of government. The cost of education is not part of municipal budgeting and has been increasingly supplemented by provincial grants. Hospital and medical care for all Canadians, regardless of age or income, is paid for under a highly effective federal-provincial scheme of national health insurance.

In Montreal's case, provincial benevolence—or authority —has proved to be an additional blessing in a time of acute embarrassment. The price of playing host to the Olympic Games in July [1976] was originally estimated at $300 million; the money was to have been raised by means of a lottery and sale of coins. Now the cost will run to at least $1.2 billion, with Mayor Jean Drapeau's "self-financing" no better than fractional. [The cost eventually reached $2 billion. —Ed.] The province, as a result, is committed to bail out Montreal. The remaining question is whether the schedule of debt repayment will cause a shutdown or slowdown of other major municipal projects. Already, the provincial government has announced a freeze on new subway work until the end of . . . [1976].

The Problem of Separatism

This contributes, in Quebec as elsewhere, to a general feeling of uneasiness, of "uncertainty." The quotation is particularly interesting since it comes from René Lévesque, the leader of the separatists, the Parti Québécois. . . . [In 1972–1973] Lévesque was convinced that the road to separatism was wide open. Since then, Quebecers have indicated their wariness of independence by giving the provincial Liberals an enormous mandate. The Parti Québécois has altered its tactics. It has said its objective can be reached in two stages: first, a victory for the party based on a program of social and economic reforms; then a referendum to decide whether French Canadians want to break away from the rest of Canada. [In November 1976 the Parti Québécois achieved one of its goals by virtue of its victory in Quebec's provincial elections. The party captured a majority of the seats in the National Assembly and its leader, René Lévesque, was elected premier.—Ed.]

It is a neat device, and attractive to those Quebecers who are not separatists but who believe the Liberal provincial government of [former] Premier Robert Bourassa . . . [was] arrogant and tainted—a description that . . . seemed particularly appropriate ever since bad meat was allowed to slip, in huge quantities, through the province's inspection system. The Parti Québécois . . . at least holds promise of providing an honest administration. . . .

The legislated push for French as the language of priority is an irritant to some English Canadians, but others recognize it as a small price to pay for confederation. Little more than five years ago the province, and the rest of Canada, was in a panic over a wave of separatist-terrorist bombings that culminated in the kidnapping of a British diplomat and the kidnap-slaying of a provincial Cabinet minister. Today the worst political crimes are insularity and apathy.

On reflection, there may be an even more heinous offense. "Mon Pays," a song written several years ago by the province's most popular *chansonnier,* Gilles Vigneault, was seized upon by separatists to become virtually Quebec's national anthem. But now, as a sign of diminished dedication or idealism, the sacred song has been souped up and turned into a commercial hit, with the rock version at the top of the discothèque lists.

LETTER FROM OTTAWA: THE SORRY STATE OF CANADIAN NATIONALISM [3]

Say what you like about Canadians, we are, historically, big givers. But what (if anything, the nationalists would say) was left to present the U.S.A. for its . . . Bicentennial? Bobby Orr is already there. So is Ottawa's very own Paul Anka. Prince Edward Island is too expensive to wrap; Baffin Island, even bigger, is bound to melt en route. And so a committee of Ottawa mandarins, backs to the wall, pondered and pondered, finally surfacing with a grabber. *A picture book.* Yes, indeed. Our government . . . allocated $1.5 million to produce a book, compiled by our leading photographers, of Canadian/American border scenes (not, one hopes, including draft dodgers sneaking home through the tall grass), and elegantly wrapped freebies . . . [for] Senators, congressmen, and small-town mayors—in fact, to most American elected officials, as well as President Ford.

Happy birthday, U.S.A., happy brithday to you! . . . You will be getting not so much a gift book as a Canadian good earth catalogue, showing what's left on the shelves, prices available from Ottawa on request.

It's not only a singularly unimaginative gift, but a grudging one. Which is to say, there's trouble out here on the tundra. The natives, reduced to tenant farmers on their own estate, grow restless. *And creative.* As witness a recent issue of *The Independencer,* a bimonthly published by a hardline nationalist faction known as the Committee for an Independent Canada. The paper displays a stirring two-page-long poem, the group inspiration of the Lorna Little Mayfield Chapter. Called "The Canadian Children's Plea," it begins:

[3] Article by Mordecai Richler, Canadian novelist, essayist, author of *The Apprenticeship of Duddy Kravitz. Harper's Magazine.* 250:28-32. Je. '75. Reprinted by permission of International Creative Management. Copyright © 1975 The Minneapolis Star & Tribune Company, Inc.

Please, Mr. Prime Minister,
    don't sell us out to the USA!
Please, Mr. Prime Minister,
    don't give our heritage away!
When we are grown and take
    our place as men and women
    of our race,
We want to be FREE—to control
    —to decide; not to the will
    of a giant tied!

No less talented is another writer prized by the inde-
pendencers, Reserve Air Force General Richard Rohmer,
our Steve Canyon, whose . . . novel, *Exxoneration,* was a
Canadian best-seller, *Exxoneration* begins where Rohmer's
earlier political dream, *Ultimatum,* ended, with the American President, at 6:30 P.M., October 7, 1980, announcing the
annexation of Canada, and our governor-general seeing no
alternative but to "follow the instructions of the President,"
even as U.S. Air Force planes are landing at all Canadian
air bases to begin occupation of the country. But wait, wait,
the imperialists' fascist bullies hadn't counted on *Exxoneration's* hero, the incomparable Pierre Thomas de Gaspé,
of whom our prime minister says, "There is something I
didn't know about, that is that de Gaspé, as well as being
president of the Canada Energy Corporation, is also your
Toronto district commander and is running Operation
Reception Party at Toronto International Airport. God,
how versatile can a man be!"

Even the Texan President of the U.S.A. respects us,
thanks to de Gaspé. "Sure the United States owns most of
the country. But those people have a fighting record in the
first world war and the second world war like you wouldn't
believe."

De Gaspé's Operation Reception Party totally defeats the
superior American invading force, and the crushed U.S. Air
Force general, just possibly a Southerner, is moved to comment: "Ah gotta hand it to you all, you sure gave it to us
good. Ah didn't know you Canadians had that much gump-

tion, but ah sure know it now and ah take my hat off to you."

Rohmer is also a master of the British idiom. The American invasion defeated, de Gaspé moved to take over Exxon, his machinations taking him to an exclusive Mayfair hotel [in London], where the valet porter awaits him. "Mr. Reimer and another gentleman are waiting for you in the sitting room, Mr. de Gaspé! Cor, you ought to see the chap with 'im. Gorblimey!"

Ultimately, the Texan President is defeated in an election by none other than David Dennis, the first Jewish President of the U.S.A., who says of his trip to Israel: "Such a welcome. For a Jewish boy from Detroit, a boy who's come up the hard way. . . ."

Rohmer's novel put me in mind of my deprived World War II boyhood in Montreal, where, with American comic books unavailable for the duration, we had to make do with our own inferior black-and-white inventions, but I should add that the sales of *Exxoneration* were prodigious for Canada, something like eighteen thousand. Even so, nationalists protest, with some justice, that the Canadian publishing industry is being swamped by the American—also with some justice, alas. For we are only some 15 million (English-speaking, that is) and you are more than 200 million, and we are dependent on American publishers for almost all the European and Asian books we receive in translation. And so, naturally enough, American publishers provide most of the books for those of us who still read for pleasure, rather than as a patriotic duty. The nationalists, however, are concerned with quantity, not quality.

The Literature Scene

Item: after my return to Canada, . . . [in 1972], it was my good luck to hear from the Committee for an Independent Canada directly. Their letter, which actually sprang from the committee's cultural think tank, began: "Dear Author, You have been chosen along with seventy-nine other major contemporary authors to present your views. . . ."

Seemingly, if on my departure for England twenty years earlier the flower of Canadian letters, like the British Liberal party, could fit snugly into a taxi, now a veritable charabanc was called for. Since then, the nationalists have made it clear that they are determined to win through legislation, for the second-rate but homegrown writer, what talent alone has hitherto denied him: an audience, applause. In 1973, they argued, of the $291 million spent on English-language books in Canada, only $15 million, to lapse into the deplorable English of *The Independencer,* was "Canadian authored and published." Furthermore, only 2 percent of the paperback books sold on the Canadian mass market are in fact written and published by Canadians, which has made things hot for Ottawa in general, Hugh Faulkner in particular. The reticent, but concerned, Faulkner . . . [was] our secretary of state, the minister responsible for cultural affairs, and in a . . . representation made to him by the militant Independent Publishers' Association, he was asked to consider, among other enormities, Canadian content quotas that would oblige bookshops and those who maintain paperback racks, as well as the foreign book clubs operating in Canada (Book-of-the-Month Club, Literary Guild), to legally display or offer as much as 20 percent Canadian content.

Following the narcotics squad, after the antisubversive division, enter the RCMP [Royal Canadian Mounted Police] paperback detail—plainclothes, of course—each constable only five-foot-four, bespectacled, checking out your corner drugstore and newsie against his Canadian content pocket calculator and if, perchance, it only registered 19 percent indigenous shlock, running them in, charged with displaying too many [Irving] Wallaces, [Harold] Robbinses, and [Jacqueline] Susanns, whilst concealing their slower-moving Canadian imitators under the counter, like condoms. Fortunately, Faulkner wouldn't buy, telling our own variation of the [Communist Chinese] Red Guard, "The right to read is basic. The Canadian public will want to read foreign books, to have access to them, and to have them reviewed in the Canadian media. Publishing is an international activity judged by international standards. Canadian publishing is necessarily judged against the output of foreign publishing, and often by the best of foreign publishing. That is as it should be." But Faulkner did come up with a concession of dubious value, a program that would make book display racks of Canadiana available in post offices. Now if, as one Ottawa wag put it, the post office handles books no better than the mail, well, well, well . . .

Meanwhile, Jack Stoddart, our only publisher of mass-market paperbacks (Paperjacks), has complained that he cannot compete with American reprint houses who are poaching here, seeking out only well-known and established authors. "If they get the top authors," he has said, "none of us will be able to afford to develop new authors." Consequently, with the surprising support of the . . . Writers' Union of Canada, he . . . called for a six-month moratorium on the sale of rights to U.S. paperback houses. Hugh Kane, vice-chairman of Macmillan, refused to subscribe. "We have," he said, "an obligation to serve our authors to the best of our ability." And, what's more, said the plainspoken Kane, the moratorium would simply protect Paperjacks, the only real Canadian presence in the field, from any competition.

Even so, I had a grudging sympathy for Stoddart's dilemma until I happened to espy one of his model contracts, wherein it appears that his concern for developing new Canadian authors is so deeply felt that, in paying for the Canadian rights, he also acquires an exclusive license to print, publish, and sell, in the U.S.A. and British Commonwealth and, fully grasping that too much bread is bad medicine for scribblers, only pays them 50 percent for these aforementioned rights. Some, admittedly, might protest Stoddart was brandishing nationalism as a shield for old-fashioned sharp practice, but this would only reveal woeful ignorance of the nationalist idiom. Look here, for an American publisher to seek Canadian rights is cultural imperial-ism, but for a Canadian to demand U.S. and Commonwealth rights, creaming 50 percent off the top, is protecting innocent colonials from foreign exploitation.

Does Anyone Care?

Content quotas, already imposed on Canadian television, have made for some talmudic conundrums. If, for instance, our Southern crackers play yours, that is to say, the Montreal Expos take to the field against the Dodgers in LA, and this is broadcast on CBC-TV, is it 100 percent Canadian content? Fifty percent? Or does it depend on the final score? Similarly, if a bona fide Canadian publisher were to bring out a book on the Philadelphia Flyers, Canadian roughnecks to the man, is this Canadian or American content?

Who knows, and who cares, was the subject of an outraged article (*Toronto Globe and Mail,* March 22, 1975) by a frequent visitor to Ottawa, one of our more impassioned, but engaging, Canada-firsters, the publisher Mel Hurtig. "One year ago," Hurtig wrote, "the Surrey-Langley chapter of the Committee for an Independent Canada conducted a 'Canadian Awareness Survey' of students in their last year of high school in six schools in and around Vancouver. When I read the results I was in turn stunned, dismayed and skeptical." For example:

☐ Fewer than 30% could identify the B.N.A. [British North America] Act as Canada's constitution. The Magna Carta, Declaration of Independence and Bill of Rights were frequent answers.

☐ 71% could not name the capital of New Brunswick.

☐ Asked to name any three Canadian authors, 61% were unable to do so. Pierre Berton was named by only 20%, Farley Mowat by 19%. All of the following were named by fewer than 5%: Eric Nicol, Leonard Cohen, Stephen Leacock, Emily Carr, Mordecai Richler, and Morley Callaghan.

Me, I'm not stunned, or dismayed. I'm flattered. For I take it that less than 5 percent of high school students in and around, say Santa Barbara, would know if Philip Roth was a delicatessen, Bernard Malamud a furrier, or Saul Bellow an orthodontist.

Something else.

One student, embarrased to have flunked his Canadian awareness test, a student whom Hurtig quotes with something like despair, I, on the other hand, applaud for redeeming himself with a quality distinctly Canadian—a self-deprecating sense of humor. His comment: "Margaret Atwood, Margaret Laurence—never heard of them, so they must be Canadian."

In Ottawa I have had my own experience of Canadian students, at Carleton University, where I was a visiting professor for two years.

One morning, early in September 1972, newly if uneasily ensconced in my professorial office, I set to interviewing applicants for the dubious course I was offering: English 298, a writing seminar. Outside my window there stretched the Rideau Canal. In the seemingly endless winter months ahead, it would be transformed into the longest and, probably, most delightful, man-made skating rink in the world, threading through the capital and its environs for four-and-a-quarter miles, providing noon-hour play not only for children, but also for civil servants and MPs. Come December, many a colleague, and even more students, would skate three miles to classes.

The students who drifted into my office that morning were engaging, and touchingly vulnerable, but I was shocked, even appalled, by how little most of them had managed to read. One young man in particular permanently endeared himself to me. I asked him, as I had all the others, "What's the last novel you read?" But this groovy Aquarian wasn't going to be conned by a loaded question from an aging writer. He pondered. He searched the ceiling; he contemplated the floor. Finally, his eyes lit with triumph, he asked: "Fiction or nonfiction?"...

"Time" for a Change

... [At l'Opéra restaurant], I dined with Marc Lalonde, one of the most astute and likable politicians in town. Lalonde, like [Pierre Elliott] Trudeau a former Montreal law professor, was for some years the prime minister's principal secretary and adviser, but has since been elected to Parliament himself, and is . . . the highly successful minister of national health and welfare. . . . [He] felt that obviously the traditional state of dependency on the U.S.A. was no longer what it was. "We've got more options," he said, "for now it's the producers of energy who can be more choosy. The continentalist energy policy," he added, "is a trap, when we are only 20 million and they are 200." But he did admit to feeling genuinely uneasy about at least one aspect of the new and, most would agree, long overdue, legislation aimed at ending the special advertising privileges of *Time* and the *Reader's Digest* in Canada.

The legislation, proposed by Hugh Faulkner, would finally do away with the provision that allows Canadian companies to deduct these advertising expenses from their income tax. This is a ruling that bona fide Canadian magazines have been ardently seeking for years, arguing that only this has prevented the development of a genuinely indigenous newsmagazine. In presenting the proposed amendment to the income-tax act, Faulkner said, "We in the government are not so much concerned with certain of the nation's industries as we are deeply committed to the nation's integrity. What happens in the area of Canadian books, magazines, and broadcasting, as in other areas of Canadian cultural expression, is not a matter of marginal interest and importance. The strength, originality, and vision we find therein is the true measure of what constitutes our national life." He also ventured, "I am confident that the enterprise and skill of the Canadian magazine industry will seize this opportunity. It is my hope and expectation that this decision will result in the creation of a Canadian newsmagazine."

As not only Hugh Faulkner, but everybody else in the House expected, Maclean-Hunter, already approaching something like a Canadian magazine monopoly, leaped hungrily into the breach, promising rather more than they are likely to deliver, a well-written newsmagazine of their own, with bureaus worldwide. This prompted one observer, the Ottawa columnist Geoffrey Stevens, to write, "The danger is that the Canadian newsmagazine industry will be transformed from a profitable U.S. monopoly to an unprofitable Canadian monopoly."

If *Time/Canada* (circulation 554,000) does disappear, undoubtedly some, if certainly not all, of its advertising income will accrue to *Maclean's,* but, alas, it will do nothing to enhance that magazine's lamentable editorial content. *Maclean's* is a supernationalist bore, the sort of booster's publication that could happily be issued by a national chamber of commerce. What with its endlessly lyrical color photographs of Canadian riverbanks, wheat fields, and barns, there is little in it but patriotism to detain any demanding reader. But, ironically, the admittedly foreign *Time,* its Canadian content limited to four to six pages, . . . for years pronounced with more authority on the state of the arts in Canada. Not a matter, *pace* Faulkner, of marginal interest or importance.

The Canadian magazine issue is fraught with embarrassments and ambiguities. Months before *Time* was directly threatened [in mid-1975], this country's oldest magazine, *Saturday Night,* self-consciously nationalist but with a good deal in it for the discerning reader, seemed to be folding, until a savior, a savior most embarrassing, emerged with the offer of a $100,000 loan. It was, whisper it, none other than Imperial Oil, that is to say, Exxon, and accepting its money was equivalent, in the good old days, to a right-wing periodical taking Moscow gold.

Even so, almost everybody supports a measure that would oblige our edition of *Time* to become more than 51 percent Canadian-owned and belatedly extend the range of its Canadian news coverage. But the ambiguity that worries Marc Lalonde, and frightens a good many others, is a rider that also says *Time*'s content must be "substantially different" from the American. And . . . [the] minister of national revenue, under whose jurisdiction the income-tax amendment falls, has explained "substantially different" as meaning 80 percent Canadian content. . . . [The minister] is reputedly a fine fellow, and just possibly he is something of a reader himself, but he wasn't elected to office for his literary prowess, or as a censor, and has no business whatsoever ordaining what we can or cannot read. Outraged, the editorial writer in the *Toronto Globe and Mail,* our most prestigious newspaper, clearly saw foreign ownership and editorial content as two distinctly separate issues. Legislating against the content of a magazine would, he wrote, "be a direct interference with the right of all Canadians to freedom in choosing. . . . Government would be defining what can be published." [A law was enacted that did end the special advertising privileges of *Time* and *Reader's Digest* in Canada, and *Time,* subsequently, discontinued its Canadian edition.—Ed.]

Not only an alarming precedent, but one that might have hilarious results, our indigenous newsmagazine, or a truncated *Time,* running endless stories about the hobbies of the mayor of Sudbury, or a traffic arrest in Nanaimo, at a moment when a war in the Middle East was threatened or Ireland was in flames. The assumption, wrongheaded and deeply insulting, is that Canadians are a parochial people.

It is also a sad, and surprising, turnabout for a government headed by Pierre Elliott Trudeau. . . . [In the mid-sixties], when he was minister of justice, Trudeau was sufficiently intrepid to sponsor a bill that made life easier for homosexuals, arguing that "the state had no business in the nation's bedrooms." Neither has it, ten years later, any business in our sitting rooms or libraries. We are quite adult enough, thank you, to decide what we want to read without any direction from the Cabinet.

The pity is that the nationalists, if they would only stay

clear of cultural matters, obviously beyond them, do, indeed, have a strong case. We are too much subject to the whims of multinational corporations, largely American-owned. It would be simply spiffy if we owned more of Canada, say, half.

Our problem, unique in the Western world, perhaps, was not an indigenous buccaneering capitalist class, indifferent to those they exploited, yet intrepid and imaginative nation-builders. Our problem was the Scots; the most inept and timorous capitalists in the West. Not builders, but vendors, or, at best, circumspect investors in insurance and trust companies.

If the pre-World War I American boy, at the age of sixteen, was dreaming of how to conquer and market the rest of the globe, his Canadian equivalent, at the same age was already seeking a position with an unrivaled pension scheme.

And so, Canadian branch plants proliferate, there's an imbalance, corrections are called for. But mindless, impassioned objection to all things American is a fool's solution. It's no answer. After all, we could eschew all things American, even the Salk [polio] vaccine, making our children "FREE—to control—to decide; not to the will of a giant tied!" Put plainly, cripples for Canada.

CANADIAN CONUNDRUMS [4]

Look out.

Canada's English-speaking writers are . . . a largely discontented, even fulminating, lot, the most militant bitterly anti-American, given to cultural paranoia, a fire sometimes stoked by real, if not necessarily malign, fatuity, as witness the review of Margaret Laurence's . . . novel, *The Diviners*, in the *New York Times Book Review* (June 23, 1974). I do not wish to quarrel with the reviewer's assessment of Mrs. Laurence's novel, which is, after all, her prerogative. But,

[4]Article by Mordecai Richler, Canadian novelist, essayist, author of *The Apprenticeship of Duddy Kravitz. American Libraries.* 6:24-7. Ja. '75. © 1975 by the American Library Association. Reprinted by permission of International Creative Management.

having once admonished Mrs. Laurence for her sloppy prose,
the reviewer sails on to place her novel in Ontario, when
it is deeply rooted in the prairie soil of Manitoba. . . . The
New York Times proper . . . was [also] guilty of a boner.
Its crossword puzzle asked for the name of an "ex-prime
minister of Canada," and the only one that fit was that of
Pierre Elliott Trudeau, who has held that office without
interruption since 1968.

Such blithely insulting ignorance of your once quiescent,
and only ostensibly boring, northern neighbour, exacerbated
by the fact that so many of our industries and natural resources are American-owned, has, understandably, created
enormous resentments in Canada.

Attention must be paid.

Look here, we not only boast a magnificent and distinctive geography, a little history all our own, singularly
honourable politicians, and an emerging, if still fragile,
indigenous culture, but, to come clean, we have long been
infiltrating your culture high, low, and middle.

Saul Bellow is a Montrealer born and has written
splendidly about his Napoleon Street boyhood in *Herzog*.
Kenneth Galbraith is also one of ours and, indeed, one of
his most engaging books, *The Scotch*, is a celebration of his
formative years in rural southern Ontario. Marshall McLu-
han, mercifully only one season's guru, is another Canadian.
We have also—shrewdly, I think—dumped Guy Lombardo
on you, as well as Robert Goulet, the California Golden
Seals and Lorne Green, the insufferably ponderous big
daddy of El Ponderosa. Why, even the makers of the Hollywood dream, Sam Goldwyn, Louis B. Mayer, and Jack
Warner, came out of Canada. And, while we're at it, please
remember that it was our steadfast rum and whisky runners
who saw you through the darkest days of prohibition.

The Question of American Dominance

But a much more deeply felt cry of anguish here [in
Canada] is that Americans are dominating our country.

Canadian politicians may differ on how to cool inflation or tackle unemployment, but they . . . lead with the elbows, outbidding each other, in promises, albeit nebulous, to buy back the country from American exploiters. I am not concerned here with the larger economic problems, real as they are, but rather with cultural conundrums, the inevitable American overspill, and how it affects the small but increasingly turbulent world of Canadian letters.

Quebec, of course, is a special case. Cocooned by language, inward-looking, it feels even more threatened by English-speaking Canada without, and foreign (that is to say, non-French-speaking) immigration within, than by American appetite, and almost . . . 41 percent of its populace voted for the separatist Parti Québécois in the . . . [1976] provincial election. Younger writers in Quebec, the most talented being novelist Roch Carrier, are largely separatist in sentiment, and many perversely consider Trudeau, and other French-Canadian intellectuals who opted for Ottawa and federalism, a sell-out. Beneath contempt.

The English-speaking Canadian's "American problem" is much more complex. Obviously, we are Americans too.

North Americans.

Ours, if you like, is the enormous attic, where, as lip-smacking, energy-starved Washington now knows, so many, many riches are stored. But for years past Canadian intellectuals, myself included, have scorned the attic's literary inventory, adjudged its standards picayune, and fled.

My good friend Robert Fulford, the editor of *Saturday Night* (incidently, the oldest as well as the most literate of Canadian monthlies), once observed the trouble with our generation of Canadians, the cultural-internationalists of the fifties, was our conviction that the only thing for the talented to do was to "graduate from Canada."

Well, yes. Certainly. But if I may repeat here an argument I first ventured in the pages of *Life* magazine, let me put the case for my generation this way.

Elsewhere—that was the operative word. The built-in insult. Canadians of my generation, sprung to adolescence during World War II, were conditioned to believe the world happened elsewhere. You apprenticed for it in Canada, on the farm with a view, and then you packed your bags and lit out for the golden cities: New York, London, Paris. Home was a good neighbourhood, but suburban, even bush, unless you happened to be a hockey player. Of all our boyhood heroes, from Joe DiMaggio to Humphrey Bogart, only hockey players were Canadian *and* undoubtedly the best. While we did have other indigenous heroes, they were badly flawed by being pint-sized versions of an altogether larger British or American presence. They were world famous—in Canada. Put plainly, any candidate for excellence was bound to be suspect unless he proved himself under alien skies. The Canadian kid who wanted to be prime minister wasn't thinking big, he was setting a limit to his ambitions rather early.

History, for us, seemed a spectator sport. Revolution, earthquakes, civil war, racial strife, famine—all were other people's miseries. We had never withstood a Spanish Armada. Or overthrown a tyrant. Why, we even lacked an Alamo. After nearly a hundred years of confederation, we remained a fragmentary country, yet to be bound by nationhood, a mythology of our own.

I am speaking of the forties now, but, as late as 1971, former Prime Minister Lester B. Pearson said to me, "We have never fought for our freedom and we have no independent political history." He recalled that when he was a young man, "We were Canadians, yes, but in a British sense; our foreign policy made on Downing Street. We emerged from World War I with a newfound pride and confidence, but just at a time when we could have built something especially our own; we fell under U.S. economic domination. Once more we failed to stand on our own feet." . . .

The Emerging Cultural Nationalism and Its Problems

Building something especially our own, hammering out a mythology, however self-consciously, is the obsession of today's young Canadian intellectuals, usually fierce nationalists. Their ardour has been fed by some heartening changes on the cultural scene and, to give them their due, has made others possible. There is, for openers, the Canada Council, its largesse so fabled that there is now no Canadian writer with even a whisper of promise who need want for a sustaining grant. There is also a National Arts Centre in Ottawa, which, certainly to my surprise, has transmogrified our nation's capital, now no longer merely a cowtown. There is the Canadian Film Development Corporation, armed with a renewable stake of ten million dollars with which to finance a fledgling industry. There's Stratford, a suddenly lively Toronto theatre scene, and a summer festival for new Canadian plays in Lennoxville, Quebec. While it's true that the Canada Council, the Film Development Corporation, and 'the National Arts Centre cannot, with all their money, actually create a uniquely Canadian culture, they do make for immensely favourable conditions.

Regrettably, the new nationalism has also fostered a good deal of embarrassing chauvinistic nonsense. If, for instance, Canadian literature was once beyond the academic pale, not studied at any of our universities, now courses on "Can. lit." abound on our campuses. Nice, very nice. But the trouble is suddenly almost everything is usable, or so it seems. Unreadable nineteenth-century writers, their talents clearly inadequate, have surfaced overnight as Canadian classics. A poor thing, but our own. Like the northern black fly. And many a journeyman contemporary novelist finds himself declared a set book only months after publication.

In the last twenty years we have come full circle, culturally.

When I started out, Morley Callaghan meant more to us than any other Canadian writer; he had been to Paris with

Hemingway and Fitzgerald and published as an equal. To us, merely apprentices at the time, it meant that it was possible to be Canadian *and* first-rate. It settled, in our minds, that if you wrote well enough about Toronto or Montreal, the larger world outside *would* pay attention. Since then Callaghan has outraged the young nationalists by saying, "Forget all about the words 'identity' and 'culture,' just never mention them. Seek only excellence and in good time people all over the world will ask about Canadians."

In Callaghan's day, of course (and in mine, too, come to think of it), respectability for a Canadian writer could only be gained by publication abroad. Today, on the new scale, to be published *only* in Canada is no longer a stigma, a measure of parochial content, but instead a badge of patriotic purity. And if a younger Callaghan were to emerge tomorrow, say out of Halifax or Regina, and accomplish as much, he would, I fear, be denounced as a turncoat, a bootlicker. There is less modesty in today's Canadian literary community, more truculence. Out of rejection, there has sprung self-pity and a certain shallow defiance. Many Canadian novelists, celebrated at home, turned down abroad, do not question their own gifts. Instead, they take this as proof of the prejudice against all things Canadian.

Nonsense.

The trouble is not with the world outside, the problem is there are far too many novels and collections of poetry being published here that could only be of interest to the writer, his family, and friends. Their outstanding merit is that they are homemade. Or, put another way, if Morley Callaghan, *pace* Edmund Wilson, was, for a period, unfairly neglected, or forgotten, abroad, other indigenous writers have been very, very fairly neglected indeed. Barely good enough for domestic use, they are frankly not for export. The sour, and to some Canadians, unacceptable truth is that, while there is arguably a measure of indifference, a lack of curiosity, there is certainly no international cabal against our novels and poetry, as witness the generous response to Hugh MacLennan, Robertson Davies, and, more recently, Richard Wright, Leonard Cohen, Margaret Atwood, and Alice Munro.

Which is not to say we don't suffer from real, essentially Canadian, disadvantages. Take, for instance, the indigenous nonfiction writer. He is, however capable, necessarily limited by the appeal of his subject matter. An American, writing a lively biography of Nixon or Kissinger, can expect to command the world's attention. Not so the Canadian journalist, say Peter Newman writing on former Prime Minister John Diefenbaker or Pierre Berton on the building of the Canadian Pacific Railway, both books prodigious domestic bestsellers, their sales abroad negligible. The Canadian publisher is also extremely vulnerable, his market impossibly small. If it's true (and possibly even obvious) to say that any of our novelists or poets who is good enough can take the entire English-speaking world for his oyster, it also must be understood that the Canadian publisher doesn't share in this potential cornucopia. His interest is limited to Canada, a market approximately one-tenth the size of the American one.

It was in recognition of this difficult situation that both the Canada Council and the Ontario Arts Council . . . rode to the rescue, bolstering our beleaguered domestic publishers with generous grants. A mixed blessing, alas. Because once the arts councils had seen to the needs of our most significant and deserving publishers, McClelland & Stewart and Macmillan, there was little else to choose from. Doubleday and McGraw-Hill Ryerson, both of whom do a decent amount of original publishing in Canada, are American owned and do not qualify for grants. For the rest, the younger publishers tend to be more impassioned than professional, and are now suffering for it. Grant money has enabled them to bid against each other for books that often don't merit publication in the first place. And now, of the smaller publishers, only the capable Mel Hurtig, of Edmonton, flourishes. Anansi is foundering and the militant New Press has gone under.

This development has not embarrassed our more ardent nationalists. Instead, they cry unfair, and have made the following demands: that . . . [by the mid-1980s] any publishing or distributing company operating in Canada be required to increase Canadian ownership and control to the standard . . . set for the broadcast industry (i.e., 80 percent) or cease to operate in Canada, that all mass-paperback distributors in Canada be required . . . [by 1977] to increase to 10 percent the percentage of Canadian-written and manufactured books displayed in every outlet, and that this percentage rise to 25 percent . . . [by 1979] and be subject to regular review.

Others would even seek to impose a Canadian content and display quota in our hardbook bookshops, which is absurd. For no sane Canadian reader's cultural needs could be satisfied, *25 percent satisfied,* by Canadian content. Put plainly, we have no such pool of talent available here yet, and content or display quotas, far from invigorating the country's cultural health, would compromise it. It would amount to nothing more than a license for the second-rate, and might drive whatever readers we have left out of the bookshops.

Neither will Canadian content quotas help our . . . aroused playwrights, now shamelessly set on gaining by stealth—or legislation, if you like—what talent alone has denied them. The Canadian playwright's mood, wrote Tom Hendry in the January 1972 issue of *Saturday Night,* has changed, "changed with a vengeance. At two conferences . . . the playwrights drew up manifestos. They demanded that theatres receiving subsidies be required to produce fifty percent Canadian material by the end of 1973." [This demand has not been met—Ed.]

God help us, is all I can say. As things stand, Canadian theatres, from the National Arts Centre, through Stratford and the rest, are pleading, scratching, digging, and weeping for acceptable, even actable, Canadian material. Hardly a month goes by when I don't hear from one or another of them asking for a play, and I daresay it's the same for many another Canadian writer. The truth is, armed with the best will in the world, our theatres still cannot find sufficient Canadian material of quality, and I defy any nationalist to show me a Canadian play of talent—no, even of promise— that lacks for a production. So I am appalled at the thought of a theatre on which a 50, or even 25, percent Canadian content quota is imposed—we haven't got the horses yet— and, in the final analysis, I must insist that Chekhov, however questionable his Canadian credentials, still has more to say to us than any Canadian playwright I can think of.

The Future of Nationalism

O Canada!

Nationalists notwithstanding, our fundamental dilemma remains unchanged over the years. Namely, is it possible to operate a decent but cautious small corner grocery of a country on the same continent as one of the most voracious of supermarket nations? Is the corner grocery worth defending? Is there anything on the shelves, but wheat, copper ore, and yearning? Is there a tradition to cherish and pass on, something more than a reputation for honest trading?

I believe there is a tradition evolving at last and that it is worth defending. But hysteria is no shield, chauvinism an unacceptable armour. Canada, Canada, count your blessings.

Because we are Canadian citizens, we have never had to acquiesce to a Suez conspiracy, on the one hand, or the obscene war in Vietnam, on the other. Somebody else's government bears the guilt-load for the suppression of freedom in Czechoslovakia. Rhodesia's not our shame, neither is Watergate. We are the progeny of a thinly populated country, basically decent, with no compromising say in the world's calumnies. This, I should think, is a moral pleasure that far outweighs our artistic shortcomings. And the same, if you like, could also be said of Sweden, Norway, and

Denmark, with one crucial difference. They are culturally sheltered by language; we, English-speaking Canadians, are not. Neither are we quite so independent.

We are, in fact, in the humiliating position of having shaken our British swaddling clothes in the thirties, not to risk the rocky road to true independence, but only to end up sucking our thumb on Uncle Sam's comfy lap, now to complain that the goodies bestowed (and eagerly consumed) have given us a stomach ache, and we are willing to regurgitate if only we can please have some of Canada back. Say half.

Providing we are willing to pay the price, which I strongly doubt, we can legislate against foreign ownership, nationalising wherever necessary, but—but—Canada cannot quite so easily pass a bill declaring indigenous pap to be soul-food, pronouncing second-rate novelists to be as necessary as Melville, Faulkner, or Fitzgerald. "There is no Canadian writer," Northrop Frye reminds us in the *Literary History of Canada,* "of whom we can say as we can say of the world's major writers, that their readers grow up inside their work without ever being aware of a circumference."

But I would like to add—no, emphasise—that there is more good and honest writing being done in Canada today than there was twenty years ago. Or, put another way, there is certainly no need to be ashamed for the neighbours. If, twenty years ago, Canadian writers suffered from neglect, what we now must guard against is over-praise at home. The largest insult. The dirty double standard. One test for Canadian writers, another, more exacting litmus applied to foreigners. I don't know, I can't be sure, but I hope I speak for everybody else in the Canadian literary house when I say either we are talented enough to pass muster, or we are not. We do not stand in need of a nationalist's dog licence. We don't want to be read in our country as village gossip because Canadians recognize the street names in our novels or can nod over the weather conditions. We wish to be read at home, and abroad, because we have something fresh to say about the human condition—or not to be read at all.

My quarrel with the nationalists is that they—obviously thinking very little of us—would put barriers above all, erecting a great cultural wall of Canada, jamming the airwaves, sealing off the frontier, sheltering us from all things American, in the slender hope that something better, something distinctly our own, would emerge from the airless land we would be left to linger in. On the other hand, it is my case that this is to twice-bless the second-rate, endorsing the mediocre merely because it's ours.

Self-indulgent cultural nationalism, lashing out at all things American, is ultimately a futile exercise. Short of scissoring the continent apart at the 49th parallel, setting Canada adrift in the Atlantic, we will continue to share it with the other Americans, and must learn to live with that, even as the U.S.A. must come to acknowledge us more generously. For, even if we gain, as I hope, a larger measure of economic independence, for redeeming our political self-respect, we will go on being culturally entwined with the United States for years to come. After all, we are twenty millions, you are two hundred; and most of us do share an English-speaking culture. The larger tradition. If we could only graciously come to terms with this—rejecting the shoddy, be it American, Canadian, or whatever—absorbing excellence wherever it springs from—then it is fair to say Canadian writers, film-makers, and other artists are in a most enviable position.

Such is the cultural yearning that the advantages and the money are out scouring the woods for us. Myth-makers are urgently needed; and, furthermore, applicants needn't be unduly inhibited. The young writer, for instance, who is settling down to a novel in the maritimes, hasn't the ghost of Faulkner peering over his shoulder. Henry James didn't come before. Or Twain. Or Fitzgerald. If the literary house is haunted, it is only by the amiable [Stephen Butler] Leacock, the dispensable [Mazo] de la Roche. For the rest, the tradition is yet to be made. It's virgin land.

II. CANADA'S POLITICAL SCENE

EDITOR'S INTRODUCTION

Canada is a nation of great diversity, and this diversity manifests itself in the Canadian political environment. In many ways the Canadian political scene can be likened to that of the United States—often characterized by divisions and infighting based upon social, economic, and sectional differences. Canadians, however, differ from Americans in regard to their respective expectations concerning what, if any, benefits should be derived from their political systems. This idea is dealt with in the first article, written by Edgar Z. Friedenberg, an American who gave up his citizenship in order to become a citizen of Canada.

The nature of Canadian government is set forth, in brief, in the section's second article, taken from the New York *Times*. The next three articles, also from the New York *Times,* present examples of some of the dilemmas currently facing Canadian politicians. The first of these three describes the problematic relationship between the federal government and the provinces based upon the division-of-power principles set forth in Canada's constitution—a document most Canadians believe needs to be amended. The next touches upon the ever present problem of bilingualism in Canadian culture, an issue described in detail in Section III below. And the final *Times* article concerns yet another disgruntled group and its demands upon the government in Ottawa: the Indians of the Northwest Territories.

A change in the political strategy of Prime Minister Pierre Elliott Trudeau is next discussed by Ian Urquhart, of the Ottawa bureau of *Maclean's* magazine. And the final selection, a press release from the Canadian embassy in Washington, DC, contains the views of several Canadian newspapers on the possibility of amending Canada's constitution—a process over which the British Parliament still retains power.

THE CANADIAN WAY: NO EXIT?[1]

I have been living near Halifax, Nova Scotia, and teaching at Dalhousie University, for nearly five years now. At the end of the fifth year, in August 1975, I shall be eligible to apply for Canadian citizenship which, if granted, would terminate my American citizenship, for the American people are a jealous prince—Canada, like Britain, accepts dual citizenship but the United States does not. This is an even greater step than most Americans believe.

Emigration, in any case, is a difficult act for most Americans to imagine—like suicide, it is embarrassing to those left behind who prefer to believe that it must have been undertaken while of unsound mind. That, surely, is what President Ford's highly publicized repatriation program for war resisters—amnesty, it isn't— . . . intended to convey. Resurrection on these terms has not proved attractive to many; and, certainly, if I am as fortunate in my *ambience* in the next world as I have been to find myself in Nova Scotia, I shall conclude that God is merciful indeed, though perhaps more merciful than just.

It has often been pointed out, as by Jessica Mitford, that Americans deal with their abhorrence of death by pretending that it is not really a major change of condition, and that the cemetery is a kind of suburb with a very low rate of violent crime and everybody on perpetual care instead of welfare. Emigration is a riskier business altogether; yet Americans think the change will be minimal for those who are only moving to Canada. Those of us who chose to leave the United States because we found its social and political policies both repugnant and deeply rooted in the nation's structure and its culture are unlikely to have made this

[1] From article by Edgar Z. Friedenberg, instructor at Dalhousie University in Halifax, Nova Scotia; author of *Coming of Age in America. Ramparts.* 13:40-4. Mr. '75. Copyright © 1975 by Edgar Z. Friedenberg. Reprinted by permission of the author.

error; if we had thought Canada would be like the United States, we would never have come here. But for most Americans emigration is unthinkable and Canada a political artifact, available as a refuge only because of the conservatism or cowardice of the people who lived in the region in 1776, but essentially similar in its customs, economic if not political institutions, and basic values.

There is just enough truth in this to be highly misleading. True, in nine of the ten provinces the natives mostly speak English; we shop in supermarkets in shopping centers; and even the Canadian Broadcasting Corporation (CBC), though a [federally owned and operated] Crown Corporation, depends on frequent and awful commercials for its short-range operating costs. True, Canadian entrepreneurs are often brasher and more vulgar versions of their American contemporaries; Sinclair Lewis characters held over miraculously for half a century. But life here *feels* totally different from the way it does in the United States; and while not all the comparisons are favorable to Canada—and whether any will be depends on what you want from life— no American who comes here to stay is likely to doubt that choosing the path less traveled by has made all the difference.

Caveat Emigrant

There are certain qualities of life that Americans are likely to miss in Canada, and these are real deficiencies. I found it especially embarrassing, having meant my departure from the United States as a political gesture as well as a search for a better life, to be forced to confront the fact that Canadians enjoy far fewer and weaker formal civil liberties than Americans do. Less than three months after my arrival here [in 1970], Prime Minister [Pierre Elliott] Trudeau had invoked the War Measures Act which suspended most civil liberties in the country for 90 days and legalized horrifying if temporary detentions *incommunicado* of key political figures in Quebec at a time when the

perfectly lawful separatist *Parti Québécois* was campaigning
for seats in a general election. The episode that led to this
proclamation was atrocious enough: the murder of a government official and the kidnaping of a British diplomat in
Quebec. But the motivations of the Liberal Government
seemed to me clearly political and it was not reassuring to
discover that 90 percent of the Canadian people approved
while John Mitchell, then U.S. Attorney General, spoke
enviously of Mr. Trudeau's powers in combatting subver-
sion. By the time the 90-day period expired, however, the
media—more elitist here than in the United States and with
no Spiro Agnew to harass them—had made the government's
action the butt of ridicule; the detainees, terrifying as their
experience had been, had long since been released; the
actual criminals who had murdered M. LaPorte and kidnapped Mr. Cross had been given safe conduct to a reluc-
tant Cuba; and the conspiracy trial undertaken by the
Crown was well on its way to ignominious collapse, occasioned by the acquittal of all but one of the alleged conspir-
ators who, as the press acidly pointed out, could hardly be
convicted of having conspired with himself. The government, in short, blew it. The most serious permanent victims
of the invocation of the War Measures Act were some
American war resisters whom the infamously authoritarian
government then in power in Vancouver—3,000 miles from
Quebec—arrested and turned over to American authorities.

Nevertheless, it is shameful that this could happen here
and did. Canada did not even pass a Bill of Rights until
1965; and it is only statute law, not a part of the Constitution and not paramount. That is, it does not automatically,
as in the United States, preempt the authority of other
statutes in cases in which there is a conflict. Each must be
decided on its merits before a notably conservative judici-
ary, and the tiny if fairly scrappy Canadian Civil Liberties
Association does not regard it as very useful. In Canada,
moreover—and this I find really shocking—there is no principle of law forbidding double jeopardy; the Crown may,

and in important cases does, appeal against an acquittal, and the accused may find himself convicted in appellate court. I could give further examples, all favorable to the United States on balance; but what they add up to is the fact that Canadians, by and large, retain a measure of basic trust in their government and have never defined it as a potentally lethal adversary against which formal and formidable defenses must be vigilantly maintained if liberty is to be preserved. I think they have learned a lot and become observably more militant during the past few years. But it must be recognized, too, that Canada did not become a nation by rejecting the authority of a putatively tyrannical government, as the United States did. It assembled itself, nearly a century later, out of colonial fragments subject to that same government, to which the United Empire Loyalists here, though by now reduced to a few nests of elderly WASPS (remarkably like the Daughters of the American Revolution), remain fiercely devoted. Upper Canada, as what is now Ontario was then called, had its revolutionary moments in the early 1840s when William Lyon Mackenzie led an unsuccessful revolt against the entrenched Orange aristocracy of the region. But there have been none since the nation itself was formed a quarter of a century later. . . .

Canadians, then, have had less practice than almost any nation in the world in learning to view their government as a real or potential evil from a consistent ideological point of view. And it has, indeed, never possessed the power to distinguish itself as an independent source of evil in the world. As Barrington Moore, Jr. pointed out in his *Reflections on the Sources of Human Misery,* nations with relatively small resources are likely to deceive themselves as to the possibilities of survival in the world while behaving decently in foreign affairs, since they are protected by the dirty work of the major power of which they are a client. That protection is dubious in that it leads to their involvement in their Godfather's affairs; but it also tends to keep them from getting blamed. Canada . . . [was] . . . notoriously supportive of American interests in the Indochina war while maintaining a posture of moral superiority that war resisters have found most convenient. The result has been that it is seldom blamed for its complicity in American aggression, and its people have been permitted to retain certain liberal beliefs—I should say illusions—about the possibility of using government to further the interests of social justice that few Americans can still hold.

This is changing. The two major Toronto dailies have . . . completed a major exposé of incidents of police brutality in that city; instances of collaboration between Canadian security forces and the CIA [Central Intelligence Agency] are now regularly exposed and readily acknowledged. Canada, unlike the United States, has an Official Secrets Act which permits government bureaucracy to conceal by investigation—that is, it creates a commission to study anything there is a public outcry about and then sits on the report which cannot be lawfully published even if somebody leaks it. But this no longer works very well. Since December 1971, when the independent journal *Canadian Forum* published substantial sections of the Gray Report—the name refers to its author rather than its style—on the domination of the Canadian economy by foreign investment after the government had withheld it for six months, aggressive reporting, especially on the CBC, has been much more notable in Canada; and though Canadian officials still waffle and procrastinate, they are having to come to terms with a rising public willingness to confront them, and a growing tendency to regard them, like politicians in the rest of the world, as unindicted co-conspirators. Their image, and perhaps their reality, is very vulnerable, since an even higher degree of collaboration between industry and government has been acceptable here than in the United States. Leftish Americans tend to regard Canada, enviously, as a nourishing hotbed of socialism; but the Canadian willingness to undertake through Crown Corporations services that in the United States would be left to private enterprise has worked largely to further private interests. Even the Government of Nova Scotia operates a public corporation called Industrial Estates, Limited, whose established function is to fund new or faltering private enterprise in the interests of creating jobs and developing the economy, thus legitimizing in this country what always seems to have to be done apologetically as a special case in the United States, as in bailing out Lockheed or Pan Am. There is also a Federal Department of Regional Economic Expansion, created in April 1969, which funds "incentive grants" to private industry at a rate up to $30,000 per job created in parts of the country deemed economically undeveloped.

If Canada moves toward a more genuine socialism, which seems to me both probable and necessary, the officials associated with these programs may find themselves, like those who worked for the CIA and its conduits in the United States in the late Fifties and early Sixties, the victims of rapidly changing social norms. In both cases, the affected cadres may claim quite justly that what they were doing was generally regarded *at the time* their programs began as not only morally justifiable but as highly progressive and well to the left of prevailing public opinion, which was one reason for being reticent about it. In matters of political morality, however, hindsight takes on a peculiarly persuasive quality; and it becomes very difficult to believe that reasonable men ought not to have known what they were doing. The subverters of Chile soon find themselves, like John Mitchell, *enchiladas;* and the men who thought they were building the economy by encouraging private investment, meanwhile establishing themselves as sound men in the minds and hearts of Canada's liberal industrial leaders, are increasingly accused of giving the nation's resources away to private investors and even supplying them the money to invest. The misconduct, however gross it may appear, that results in political scandals seldom turns out to have been greatly in violation of the norms that prevailed at the time the scandalous behavior began. What happens is that politicians fail to notice that norms have changed, since they surround themselves as far as possible with like-minded lieutenants; and they cannot in any case extricate themselves from long-range commitments that are proving disastrous. Canada, I rather think, may be heading into a series of such storms. Though by American standards they will be tempests in a teapot, tea is still an important beverage here as it was, in earlier days, in Boston. Canadian officials have long been lulled by lavish allotments of legitimacy; their withdrawal symptoms may be rather ugly.

A Quality of Life

All this has been meant as a form of stipulation: let it be agreed, before the discussion proceeds, that this is not only an imperfect nation, but that there are no formal grounds for regarding it as a society morally superior to that of the United States. Nor do immigration patterns suggest a consensus on this point. While, for the past few years, the absolute net balance of migration between the two countries has been northward, a far larger *proportion* of Canadians still emigrate to the United States than vice versa—though growing restrictions on immigration to either country in response to economic difficulties of the Western world are making such comparisons meaningless as indicators of how people feel. Nevertheless, invigorating as I find visits to the United States to be, I have never returned to Canada without an immediate and substantial sense of improved well-being. This is not euphoria, such as I used to feel going back to the University of California at Davis during my first two years there, before the sheer malevolence of the government of California and the Regents of the University freaked me out—such a rich and beautiful place, and so promising. Returning to Canada from the United States is more like the first fever-free day after a hectic illness. I just want to relax and feel sustained by a lower-keyed and more humanly-scaled environment. This is true even when I am not coming from New York, but from rural northern Minnesota, where I was on my last journey to the States. It isn't that the place is so crowded; it's the way the people come on as if the world were an unending convention and they had one eye on your name tag to see if you were important, because they had no way of knowing from listening to what you said, which they had no intention of doing anyway. The first thing I notice when I come *to* the States is that my assumptions about conversation which work in Canada are naive there. In Canada, if people ask you a question, they wait for you to answer it—though, as I have indicated, if you are a government official they may grow impatient after the first six months. In the United States, they don't; they interrupt you to talk about something else if you try.

In part, this really is because there are too many people; even if the particular scene you're in at the time is not crowded, the people who are there have trained themselves to compete against a very large and competitive field and act accordingly. The experience of American cities today is really something else; and to encounter it raises some rather curious and unexpected questions in my mind about basic democratic polity, akin to the questions abortion raises in the minds of Catholics concerned about the soul of the fetus. Were *all* these people really endowed by their Creator with certain unalienable rights? If so, what did they do with them? And what was the instrument by which so priceless an endowment was conveyed? Can you really count on copulation to do that, every time, even though this is rarely the intent? It doesn't seem to be working out.

Canada, which makes more modest promises and arouses lesser hopes, is less riven by anguish and torn by rage, though there is quite a bit of petty malice. Anger is not the basic context of life here; indeed, there is too little; the people have been trained to be docile. Canadian schools are even more oppressive than American schools, though physically safer; and this is the first year since I've been teaching here when my students, even in the University, have mostly felt free to talk back. (Maybe they're just beginning to really believe I like it; maybe, too, we're on a different part of the curve from the United States, where reports from the campuses indicate that there is now widespread satisfaction among administrators at the diligence and grade-grubbing of the students of the Seventies. The editors of *Change: The Magazine of Higher Learning*, the professional journal, or house organ, of the American university industry, to take a notable example, often sound like *Rigoletto* exulting over the assassination of the wicked Duke, before he looks at the body.)

For the first few years here, I was quite impatient with what seemed to me the passivity of the Canadian people in the face of obvious exploitation by local elites and by Americans acting through them. Meanwhile, as usual, everything was changing including me. Canadians were getting more impatient and outspoken, and certainly no one would accuse them today of being docile in their attitude toward American domination, real or fancied. And I was coming to see that I had misinterpreted a vital aspect of Canadian socialization. What I had taken for docility was not just the consequence of having been trained to inhibit one's resistance to authority—though there is still too much such discipline. It is also the consequence of *not* having been trained to believe that one is, or ought to be, the master of the universe, to whose technical wizardry in the social and natural sciences all difficulties should yield. Americans, I am . . . frequently informed, are freaking out in large numbers because they are increasingly aware that they do not know how to solve their social problems: poverty, unemployment, racism, crime in the streets. But in Nova Scotia, these aren't problems; they're what we've got; though not, as with nicer things, in quite the abundance that Americans have come to expect. Nobody expects them to go away. Meanwhile, our lives go on; our friends drop in, not unexpectedly; they may not phone but, then, we are familiar with their habits. Most of the people we deal with know who we are.

Not much of this, I am sure, can be true of Toronto or Vancouver. Yet even these cities are still coherent in a sense in which major American cities no longer are. Toronto . . . re-elected, sweepingly, a mayor who had earlier sponsored a bill limiting new construction to a height of 45 feet, against the opposition of a powerfully organized construction industry; while New York City, the last I heard, had not even been able to regain from the State the authority to inspect nursing homes and condemn them for violation of health and safety regulations. Canadians are not good at Final Solutions but they are much better at defining and attacking specific and legitimate problems. Indeed, one of the greatest threats to the Canadian way of life lies, I think, in the fact that Canadian success in solving problems within the limits of its political system may lead Canadians to retain their faith in liberalism, and even Liberalism, until it is simply too late, in a time of apocalypse, to resolve pressing moral dilemmas related to welfare and liberty. The Canadian system of social services is so much more fully developed than the American that it is difficult for most people here to realize either how inadequate it still is—that is, how poor the poor still are—or how much it has encroached on individual freedom already. The social-worker mentality can be a real threat to the freedom not only of the poor here—as in America—but to the middle classes as well. A declining faith in legitimacy may lead the body politic to develop a healthier resistance to the meliorist intrusions of authority; but it cannot take the place of a genuine reassessment of social priorities in which the claims of welfare and of liberty are coolly contrasted. This has never been done in either Canada or in the United States, which has suffered a precipitous loss in the physical quality of life without compensating gains in either community or individual freedom—indeed, it is the simultaneous loss of all these things that is terrifying. To many Americans, this terror manifests itself as a fear of becoming the victim of senseless violence; but violence is a perfectly sensible way of treating objects you do not value, and whose possible humanity does not concern you; especially in a society that has always cherished violence as an instrument of political coercion and legitimized it until its institutions lost their power to legitimize anything. Nothing has happened, or will happen, in the streets of New York that William Butler Yeats did not predict in a single, familiar poem—though one might have expected a more impressive rough beast than Gerald Ford, . . . slouching toward Washington to be born.

HOW CANADA IS GOVERNED [2]
Sovereign and Head of State

The Queen [of England], whose authority is exercised by the governor general who is appointed on the advice of the Federal Government.

The Courts

The Supreme Court of Canada is not written into the Constitution as in the United States, but established by act of the Canadian Parliament. The nine judges are appointed by the Federal Government. Three must be from Quebec because Quebec uses a French type of Civil Code different from the English Common Law used in the other nine provinces. The Supreme Court has appellate jurisdiction in civil and criminal cases throughout Canada and now exercises jurisdiction in constitutional matters. Provincial superior and county court judges are named by the Federal Government.

The Federal Parliament

House of Commons of 264 members, the delegation from each province based on population. The two largest delegations are Ontario's 88 and Quebec's 74. Term is for 5 years unless the House is dissolved sooner.

Senate of 104 members, appointed by the governor general on the advice of the Federal Government. Term of the

[2] Adapted from material in New York *Times*. p E 2. N. 21, '76. © 1976 by The New York Times Company. Reprinted by permission.

appointment is until age 75. Senators must be 30 years of age and must have property worth $4,000 in the province for which they are appointed. Representation, not based on population, is weighted to favor smaller constituent units. Quebec has 24 Senators, Ontario 24.

The Federal Government

Following the British tradition, the Government is usually formed by the party winning the largest number of districts in a general election. Usually it has a majority of seats. Formally, the governor general asks the leader of the winning party to [assume the position of prime minister and] form a Cabinet which is approved by a vote of confidence in the Commons. The Government continues in office as long as it has the support of a majority in the Commons. If it loses that support, the governor general can turn to the leader of another party who has that support or he can dissolve Parliament and an election follows. Under the British North America Act, the British legislation that serves as Canada's constitution, the Federal Government has authority over defense, customs and excise, foreign relations, money and banking, unemployment insurance, criminal law, broadcasting, agriculture and immigration, old age and disability pensions, and all matters not specifically allocated to provincial jurisdiction. (The provinces also have some jurisdiction in agriculture, immigration and pension fields, but Federal law prevails in cases of conflict.)

The Provincial Governments

The Queen is represented in each province by a lieutenant governor, named on the advice of the Federal Government.

Each of the 10 provinces has its own elected legislature. The provincial governments are chosen by the same formula as the Federal Government. The two Territories (Yukon and Northwest) are governed by commissioners (appointed by the Federal Government) and elected councils.

The provincial governments exercise powers over direct taxation within the province, administration of justice and provincial prisons, administration of property and civil rights, education, agriculture, some aspects of immigration, and minor matters such as licensing businesses. By comparison with American states, they have much broader powers.

AN UNEASY ALLIANCE: CANADA AND ITS PROVINCES [3]

Two French Canadians are to meet . . . [in December 1976] in one of the more dramatic confrontations in modern Canadian history. Pierre Elliott Trudeau, whose home town is Montreal, is prime minister of Canada and is responsible for maintaining its territorial integrity. René Lévesque, whose home town is also Montreal, is premier-elect of Quebec after last week's [November 1976] election, and he wants to lead his province eventually to independence.

Both men are governing under extraordinarily complicated and delicate arrangements. Canada is commonly, and rightly, thought of as a sovereign nation able to make its own decisions in foreign and internal matters. Yet, Canada's basic constitution is not in Ottawa but in London where, moreover, its chief of state resides. Queen Elizabeth's rule over Canada is more symbolic than anything else, but what is not symbolic is the British North America Act of 1867, which remains the basic charter of the Canadian nation.

The Quebec election involved more than just a change of parties and government. Because the Parti Québécois has as its fundamental option the independence of Quebec, suddenly the rest of Canada must look on Quebec in a different light. But Mr. Lévesque must not only deal with Canada but with Britain as well. And Queen Elizabeth is thrust into the role of George III trying to stave off a form of rebellion on the North American continent.

[3] Article by Henry Giniger, staff correspondent based in Montreal. New York Times. p E 2. N. 21, '76. © 1976 by The New York Times Company. Reprinted by permission.

In each Canada Yearbook summarizing the state of the Canadian nation at the end of every year, there appears the following explanation of Canada's constitutional arrangement:

Although the essential principles of cabinet government are based in custom or in constitutional usage, the Federal structure of Canadian government rests on the explicit written provisions of the British North America Act. Apart from the creation of a Federal union, the dominant feature of the act and indeed of the Canadian federation was the distribution of powers between the central or Federal government on the one hand and the component provincial governments on the other. In brief, the primary purpose was to grant to the Parliament of Canada legislative jurisdiction over all subjects of common interest while giving to the provincial legislatures jurisdiction over all matters of local or particular interest.

Provincial jurisdiction extends to such matters as schools, roads, urban affairs and social welfare. The provinces have taxing powers equal to the Federal Government in a direct field but are restricted as far as indirect taxation is concerned. Quebec and other provinces depend on Ottawa to finance many of their programs and this dependency creates resentments because it restricts local freedoms. The provinces can to a considerable extent set their own economic and social policies including the establishment of minimum wages and conditions governing investments. But, as in the United States, such matters as defense and foreign affairs, including the setting of tariffs are Federal responsibilities as are communications, including the licensing of radio and television stations.

Following World War II, in which the Federal Government gathered greater power to itself, there has been an increasing tendency on the part of the provinces to want more autonomy. This tendency is accelerated by the political diversity of Canada's governments. The Liberal Party is in power in Ottawa but differs in philosophy from the Conservative and Socialist regimes in power in some provinces and, even from the departing Liberal regime in Quebec. In

Quebec, the Liberal Party is run independently of the federal Liberal Party although many persons belong to both. The separation occurred in 1960 as a result of an upsurge of nationalism in Quebec.

The history of the federation since the act was passed is consequently one of tension between the Federal power in Ottawa and the local power in what has been, since 1949, 10 provinces. Nowhere has this tension been greater than between Ottawa and Quebec because of the simple difference between the English-speaking majority on the one hand and the French-speaking minority on the other.

Ever since Britain defeated France on the Plains of Abraham above Quebec City in 1756, French Quebec has felt the need to defend itself against English power whether in Ottawa or in London. Quebec governments have traditionally sought to widen their powers at the expense of the Federal Government. This will now be more true than ever with the Parti Québécois in power. The party has served notice that it intends to begin a step-by-step negotiation with Ottawa to increase local responsibility. In the immediate future, the province wants control over the Social Security system in which hundreds of millions of dollars are at stake, and over immigration policy because that policy will help determine whether French Canada remains French or not. [For additional discussion of the Quebec dilemma, see Section III, Quebec and Canadian Unity, below.]

These issues have been debated for some time, as moves have been under way to "bring Canada's constitution home" by substituting a Canadian document for the British act. The moves have been stymied to a large extent [because of the] failure of the provinces to agree among themselves over what powers they want.

Just so long as the British act prevails, Ottawa does not have a completely free hand. The original British North America Act made no provision for amendment of Canada's constitutional arrangements by any legislative authority in Canada. In 1949, the power of the Canadian Parliament to amend the constitution was established except for matters concerning the legislative authority of the provinces and the rights and privileges of provincial legislatures or governments. There continues to be no provision in the act for secession.

Even assuming the best will in the world in Ottawa toward Quebec's demands—a big assumption right now, given Mr. Trudeau's determination to show that he is one French Canadian who does not want to break up Canada—Quebec at one point or other will have to deal not only with Ottawa but with the British House of Commons. From all reports, Westminster is not in the mood to preside over the liquidation of the Canadian federation.

Would there be an Abraham Lincoln in Ottawa to fight a civil war over the issue and a George III in London to put down a rebellion against the Crown? Both eventualities are more than doubtful and all sides may then come around to a more amiable conception of Quebec's place on the North American continent. The major concern for Ottawa and London is that not only Quebec is involved. Other provinces, with strong economic ties to the United States, may also succumb to the same temptation as Quebec. The British North America Act has been amended 14 times by the British Parliament. The 15th will surely be the hardest.

THE ROLE OF BILINGUALISM IN POLITICS [4]

French-speaking air traffic controllers of Quebec Province announced on . . . [August 26, 1976] that they will seek federal recognition as a separate aviation union, breaking their present affiliation with the Canadian Air Traffic Control Association, the national union with a majority of English-speaking members. The Quebec controllers have gone so far as to enlist the support of larger French-speaking labor groups, including the militant Quebec Teachers Fed-

[4] From "Canada: More at Stake Than the Language," by Robert Trumbull, staff correspondent based in Ottawa. New York Times. p E 3. Ag. 29, '76. © 1976 by The New York Times Company. Reprinted by permission.

eration, making this the latest in a series of confrontations over language that, in the words of Prime Minister Pierre Elliott Trudeau, have raised serious issues of "national unity."

The linguistic rivalry in Canada, with the French faction about 27 percent of the population, is the most overt expression of a historic cleavage between the cultural descendants of the early French settlers, who were the first white colonists . . . , and their English conquerors. Under the umbrella issue of language, the French-speaking community is struggling to preserve Gallic culture in Canada against the pressure of English. Facing superior economic forces, and steadily losing in numbers for various reasons, including a declining birth rate in Quebec, the French Canadians see themselves as "a French island in an English sea."

Unless checked, according to Mr. Trudeau, the language dispute could lead to the departure of French-speaking Quebec from the Canadian Federation, or at least greatly encourage the long-standing independence movement by Quebec separatists, a growing minority in Canada's largest province. [In the November 1976 provincial elections in Quebec, the Parti Québécois captured the premiership and a majority of the seats in the provincial legislature.—Ed.]

In Quebec, if nowhere else in Canada, the French have more than held their own in cultural fields. The French-language theater thrives in the province, which includes Canada's most populous city of Montreal, as do French television, radio, books, magazines, newspapers and movie industry that far outstrips its English-language rival. Language is the life, as well as the symbol, of the French struggle. Prime Minister Trudeau, a Montrealer, came to power in 1968 on a pledge to enforce bilingualism in public service. French political power in Ottawa is immense, with 74 Quebec seats in a Parliament of 264 members.

Central to the conflict is the "English backlash." In most of the country where French is seldom if ever heard, the indignant cry of many English-speaking Canadians is that

French is being "rammed down our throats." Resentments are exacerbated by linguist anomalies. There is a critical shortage of English-speaking nurses in Montreal because English-speaking applicants cannot pass the French language test required to practice the profession there.

Prime Minister Trudeau was only the third prime minister from French Canada in a century. Understanding the relation of the linguistic question to Quebec separatism, he pushed through the official language act of 1969, which guaranteed equality of French and English in federal functions. But the act, intended to reassure the French, generated additional resentment among the English. People in English-speaking communities ridiculed the regulations requiring labels in French as well as English on the stocks in their stores. English-speaking civil servants resented having to study French, even though at Government expense, if they hoped to reach the upper levels in federal employment.

Around the same time, Premier Robert Bourassa of Quebec, [ousted in the 1976 provincial elections], who viewed the soothing of French Canadians on the language issue as a way of diffusing the separatist appeal, pressed through a law making French the only official language of the province. This aroused intense hostility among the English-speaking Quebeckers, who are now forbidden to use their own language in business with the Government.

At the same time French Canadians were inflamed by the slighting of their language on the local levels in predominantly English-speaking provinces such as Ontario. A university professor in Ottawa refused to register his child for a birth certificate issued in English only. A number of French Canadians went to jail for a day or two rather than pay fines for minor traffic citations issued in English. Any incident which disparaged a French Canadian—such as the series of recent scandals implicating cabinet members with French names—might be interpreted as evidence of an anti-French plot. Many English Canadians chafed over what they conceived to be the emergence of "French power" in

Ottawa under Mr. Trudeau, whose closest associates in the cabinet also happen to be Quebeckers.

Meanwhile the *Parti Québécois,* which advocates independence for Quebec, appeared to be gaining strength. It won . . . [41] percent of the popular vote in the . . . [1976] Quebec election, a substantial gain. . . .

The Roots of the Conflict

The roots of the conflict go back to old rivalries in Canada between Britain and France. Britain won the territorial struggle more than two centuries ago in a climactic battle on the Plains of Abraham, now a Quebec City park and tourist attraction. With the debacle on the Plains of Abraham, the French aristocrats and wealthy entrepreneurs went back to France with the defeated troops. The former French Canada was left peopled mostly by peasants.

The bulk of French Canadians drifted into lower occupations and tended to congregate in French-speaking ghettos. Class barriers arose between the two communities and the situation reached a crisis point during World War II when French Canadians objected to being drafted to fight alongside British Canadians. William Lyon Mackenzie King, the prime minister at the time, declared in his . . . wartime diaries that the country had been on the verge of civil war when the victory in Europe ended the episode.

In this charged atmosphere, the organized airline pilots and the [non-French-speaking] air traffic controllers refuse to countenance a broader use of French in Quebec airports, beyond the five small ones where it is already in use, on grounds of safety. A strike . . . [in July 1976] by the controllers was halted by an injunction. The pilots, ignoring a similar court action, refused to fly for nine days. [The implementation of the plan to extend the use of French to air traffic control towers has been postponed pending the results of a safety study.—Ed.]

The controversy swiftly burst through the parameters of an aviation safety discussion. The two sides exchanged accusations of "bigotry" and "racism" in the newspapers, on television and in the radio open line shows across the country on a scale that Mr. Trudeau says is unprecedented in his experience. Not the least of Mr. Trudeau's concerns is the possibility of having to fight an election on the question of bilingualism within the next two years, and the risk of generating further heat between the two groups.

AN INDIAN PROVINCE? [5]

Leaders of the 7,000 Indians of the Northwest Territories filed a formal demand with the Government . . . for ownership rights and separate political jurisdiction over 450,000 square miles of the federally administered area.

Earlier, spokesmen for 15,000 Eskimos in the Canadian North had asked that 750,000 square miles be made into a separate province. If both claims are granted by Ottawa, more than a third of Canada would revert to government by the indigenous peoples.

In documents handed to the minister for Indian and northern affairs, Warren Allmand, the Indians asked that the area of their claim be placed under the jurisdiction of a new political entity, equivalent to a province, to be known as the Dene nation.

Dene—pronounced DEN-nay, it is an Indian word meaning the people—was adopted as the name of the proposed province by the Indian Brotherhood of the Northwest Territories.

George Erasmus, president of the brotherhood, in presenting the claims to Mr. Allmand . . . , declared that the Indians of the North wished to function politically as "a nation within Canada."

"We would see our government roughly equivalent in status to the provincial level," he explained. "In no way are we challenging the legitimate jurisdiction of the federal government."

[5] From a news report entitled "Indians Ask Canada for a Province." New York *Times*. p 3. O. 26, '76. © 1976 by The New York Times Company. Reprinted by permission.

The area claimed by the Indians, who belong to several tribes, is confined mostly to the Mackenzie River Valley and includes all the Northwest Territories not claimed by the Eskimos in their presentation to the Government last February [1976].

The Eskimo claim takes in all of the land above the tree line, where the forest gives way to the Arctic wasteland. The Eskimos asked for a province of their own, to be called New Nunavut. The Eskimo word, pronounced noo-NAH-voot, means "our land."

About 16,000 whites and people of mixed blood also live in the Northwest Territories; many of the whites are temporary residents employed by the Government, private companies or missions.

Mr. Erasmus, speaking for the Indians, asserted that the proposed agreement on land claims and political rights submitted to the Government would replace Indian rights lost in earlier treaties.

"We are calling for a radical change in the relationship between aboriginal people and the people of Canada," he said. "Furthermore, we do not see why our right to self-determination cannot be met within the Canadian Confederation."

TRUDEAU'S NEW STRATEGY [6]

Prime Minister Pierre Trudeau was paying penance. He sat in a small meeting hall near Charlottetown listening to Prince Edward Island [PEI] businessmen and farmers reel off complaints against his government: high energy costs, milk-production quotas, a doubling of ferry rates to the mainland, poor rail service. Outside, PEI unionists were getting into the mood for organized labor's October 14 [1976] day of protest against wage and price controls by picketing the hall. Inside, Trudeau listened, but promised no miracles.

[6] From "The Return of a Man Called Trudeau," by Ian Urquhart, a member of *Maclean's* Ottawa bureau. *Maclean's.* 89:22+. O. 4, '76. Copyright © 1976 by Maclean-Hunter, Limited. Reprinted with permission.

Battling to overcome the Liberals' increasingly grim showing in the polls, Trudeau late in September [1976], embarked on the first of a series of fence-mending missions with a five-day swing through the Maritimes [Nova Scotia, New Brunswick, and Prince Edward Island] that took him to some 12 cities and towns. In the course of his journey, he was called a bum by organized labor, described as arrogant and uncaring by angry housewives, and told by fishermen, farmers and tourist operators that his economic, farm and transport policies are causing havoc. There were, to be sure, flashes of the old Trudeaumania, particularly in northern New Brunswick, which is French Canadian and solidly Liberal. At Tracadie, there was a 1968-style mob scene as Mounties strained to hold back a crowd of about 500 surging around Trudeau. But elsewhere, the PM [prime minister] seemed to shun the contact and kept to his hotel room for hours on end.

If Trudeau succeeds in reversing the Liberals' downward spin in the polls, he will probably run again in the 1978 election. But if he fails, the Liberals will almost certainly move to deprive him of the opportunity by opting for a new leader, probably former finance minister John Turner.

Trudeau's strategy is twofold: first, he and his ministers plan to travel more to meet people, including disgruntled Liberal Party workers, and they will try to put a new gloss on the government's tarnished image. Two major sources of countrywide discontent, bilingualism and wage and price controls, will receive special attention. Back in Ottawa, the second tactical thrust will be a deliberate attempt to slow down the pace of change and emphasize consolidation. The "new society," that awesome phrase that frightened so many, is apparently dead just nine months after it was first uttered by Trudeau in his now famous [1975] year-end television interview.

As a necessary prelude to his attempt to retrieve lost ground, the beleaguered Trudeau presided over a cabinet shuffle of a magnitude that caught Ottawa by surprise, generally pleased the business community and seemed to signal a tilt to the right. The shuffle also served to increase still further Trudeau's domination of the cabinet. The past year [1976] had seen the departure from the cabinet of three veteran ministers—John Turner, Jean Marchand and Gérard Pelletier. Now two more long-serving ministers, House Leader Mitchell Sharp and C. M. (Bud) Drury, the minister of science and technology who doubled as public works minister, stepped aside to help make way for seven new and generally younger faces in cabinet.

The shuffle also resulted in the unexpected departure of cabinet veteran Bryce Mackasey following an emotional showdown with Trudeau. The shuffle nearly cost Trudeau the services of Allan MacEachen, who agreed reluctantly to give up the external affairs portfolio to replace Sharp as house leader, where his skill in parliamentary manoeuvering will be needed by the government during the difficult months ahead. A gloomy MacEachen confided to a friend: "I felt I was just getting it all together at External."

At least three of Trudeau's new appointments won a warm reception in the business community. One was the choice of Anthony Abbott to take over at Corporate and Consumer Affairs, a somewhat improbable choice forced on Trudeau by Mackasey's last-minute departure from the cabinet. Tony Abbott's father, Douglas, was [Prime Minister William Lyon] Mackenzie King's finance minister, and the younger Abbott is a former head of the Retail Council of Canada, the lobby for the major department stores and supermarket chains. In his new portfolio, Abbott will be responsible for legislation he once lobbied against, including the competition bill. The Retail Council naturally greeted his appointment with delight, while the Consumers' Association of Canada expressed "extreme disappointment" at Mackasey's departure. Insisted Abbott: "I want to set aside the notion that I'm a running dog of capitalism."

Other moves applauded by business included the appointment of Jean Chrétien, who had earned a reputation as the "Mr. No" on government spending as president of the treasury board, to head Industry, Trade and Commerce, and the choice of Len Marchand, the first native Canadian in the federal cabinet, as minister responsible for small business, a new portfolio. The new man at External Affairs is Newfoundland's Don Jamieson, a portly pitchman who is considered relatively pro-American and will be given the job of trying to mollify American businessmen made uneasy by nationalist tendencies in the Trudeau government.

Some of Trudeau's other appointments appeared to favor the progressive wing of the party, most notably the shift of Warren Allmand from solicitor general to Indian and Northern Affairs. Allmand, who admits to a bias in favor of Canada's native peoples, replaced Judd Buchanan, who succeeded in alienating most native leaders during barely two years in the portfolio. Bud [Jack Sydney George] Cullen, promoted from the Department of Revenue to the immigration portfolio to replace Robert Andras who went to the Treasury Board, Francis Fox, named solicitor general in place of Allmand, and John Roberts, who replaces Hugh Faulkner as secretary of state, are all considered progressives. Trudeau also moved to soften the anti-French backlash in the country with the appointment of Andras, a comparative cabinet veteran, to the Treasury Board, where he will also be responsible for bilingualism. Andras, an anglophone with a reputation for cooling off troublespots, can be expected to draw less fire as overseer of federal bilingualism policies than did Chrétien, a Quebec francophone. Trudeau also moved to protect his right flank by appointing Iona Campagnola, a British Columbia MP who favors hanging and opposes gun controls, as minister responsible for sports.

The political coloration of the new cabinet was in keeping with the sombre and generally conservative mood that prevails in prime ministerial circles these days.

Accordingly, the government's Throne Speech at the opening of the new session of parliament in mid-October will probably be an understated document, emphasizing

industrial productivity and economic growth. Unemployment, the forgotten problem, will receive attention, but
bold new initiatives and socially oriented legislation will be
scarce. The proposed competition bill, part two, will be
highlighted, but that legislation is essentially five years old
and is meant to encourage free enterprise, not kill it. The
bilingualism program will likely be altered slightly to put
more emphasis on teaching the young, as recommended last
spring [1976] by Official Languages Commissioner Keith
Spicer. A new immigration law is expected to reflect the
conservative mood of the country by further tightening
entrance requirements. [This political scenario has—as of
early 1977—been acted out almost exactly as predicted.—
Ed.]

Trudeau's advisers are also hard at work on the Liberal
image—to the point that some party members fear that real
issues may get lost in the process. Now senior Liberals are
expressing concern that the government, instead, should be
getting ready for the tough decisions that loom ahead on
such complex issues as the proposed Mackenzie Valley
natural gas pipeline, the balance of payments problem and
native rights. Says a former ministerial aide: "The feeling
seems to be: when in trouble, advertise."

AMENDING CANADA'S "CONSTITUTION" [7]

On the first and second of October [1976] the provincial
premiers met in Toronto to attempt to find an acceptable
formula for amending the British North America Act, Canada's "constitution." The B.N.A. was adopted by the British
Parliament in 1867. Because the provinces and the federal
government have not been able to agree on an amending
process, the British Parliament still retains that power.
Prime Minister [Pierre Elliott] Trudeau has said that his
government will remove the B.N.A. from British control

[7] From "Patriating the British North America Act." (Press Release no 36)
Canadian Embassy. Public Affairs Division. 1771 N St. N.W. Washington, DC
20036. '76.

even if the provinces cannot agree on an amending formula.

One frequently suggested formula, developed at the 1971 Victoria, British Columbia, federal-provincial conference, would require for amendment the consent of the Canadian Parliament, the Provinces of Quebec and Ontario, two Western Provinces with 50 per cent of the western population, and two of the Atlantic Provinces. Quebec backed out of that agreement, and now the provinces are faced with another stumbling block. Premier [Peter] Lougheed of Alberta has insisted that amendment be allowed only with the unanimous consent of the provinces. In Toronto, Premier Lougheed stuck by his proposal and no agreement was reached.

□ The *Toronto Star* (October 1) favoured the Victoria conference formula: "The present system, under which the British North America Act can only be legally changed by an act of the British Parliament, is embarrassing to Canadians. No sovereign state should require another's consent to alter its own fundamental law. But patriation would be merely symbolic unless it was accompanied by a fair and rational method by which the constitution can be amended in Canada. It is in devising such a method that the catch has always come. . . . The best method for amending the constitution is the one worked out at the 1971 Victoria conference, chaired by Trudeau and attended by all the provincial premiers. . . . What provincial leaders need to remember is that the constitution cannot be kept frozen in a time of rapid economic and social change. If we cannot work out a formal method of amendment, changes will come by some other means. It may be arbitrary, unilateral action by the federal government in some national emergency. Or . . . the courts may do the changing, "interpreting" the British North America Act in ways its authors never dreamed of—as the U.S. Supreme Court has so often done. Surely it is better that the changes should come through an open, orderly system of amendment in which every part of Canada will have a voice. It is up to the 10 premiers to show some statesmanship and let Canada bring home a workable constitution."

☐ *Le Devoir* of Montreal (October 1) hoped for a common solution to the constitutional question: "Quebec is not a province like other provinces. As long as it continues to be a part of Canada, it has, nonetheless, an interest in cooperating with the other provinces in trying to find common positions on the constitution. To this end, the Toronto conference gives it an opportunity for dialogue which it must not miss. One hopes fervently that the result will be a provincial agreement which could in its turn facilitate the realization, under the best conditions, of Mr. Trudeau's master plan which, with good reason, calls for a completely Canadian constitution as soon as possible."

☐ The *Winnipeg Free Press* (October 1) criticized Trudeau's suggestions for an interim solution: "In these circumstances, the prime minister would be well advised to re-examine his own position in the event that the provinces remain divided. He has argued, and quite rightly, that Parliament would not be helpless in these circumstances but might move, independently, to make the constitution amendable in Canada. There has been criticism that such action would be unwise: that it would aggravate existing federal-provincial difficulties. But a more serious objection arises from the specifics of Mr. Trudeau's proposal. For in outlining various choices, he has sought to diminish opposition by proposing an interim arrangement—pending agreement on an amending formula, any substantive change would require the consent of the 11 governments and legislatures. . . . The prime minister is in danger of becoming the prisoner of his own project. He has been at the head of the movement for constitutional reform. But the last thing he can have desired is a "dead" constitution: one so locked in vetoes that change becomes a practical impossibility. An interim agreement, without time limit, would enable provinces making extreme demands to obtain what they could never secure through negotiations."

☐ The *Montreal Star* (September 30) considered [for-

mer] Quebec Premier Robert Bourassa's position on amending the B.N.A.: "Premier Bourassa has given indications
that a formula may be found to meet Quebec's demands for
cultural protection. Mr. Bourassa's problems are unique. In
constitutional controversy in this province, it is always
easier to be against rather than for. No Quebec government
will lose points for standing up against constitutional proposals which it claims to be against the province's interests.
Any agreement, on the other hand, no matter how favorable,
is bound to find critics who will accuse the premier of selling
out. If Mr. Bourassa is, as rumored, planning a general
election this fall [1976], that consideration must lie heavily."
[Mr. Bourassa did run for reelection in the November 1976
provincial elections, and was defeated.—Ed.]

☐ The *Ottawa Citizen* (October 1) linked economic
problems with unfavourable prospects for successful talks:
"Worldwide recession and inflation have clouded the future
for the entire country, which, as these constitutional talks
prove, is more a collection of self-interested states than a
national entity. The federal government will ask the British
government for the B.N.A. Act with or without a formula
from the provinces. Maybe having the power to amend our
own constitution will provide a sense of national identity,
but the greater likelihood is that once it is here there will
be just as much wrangling as before."

☐ *La Presse* of Montreal (October 4) tried to discern
Premier Bourassa's intentions after the Toronto meeting:
" 'What will happen if Mr. Trudeau acts unilaterally? It is
impossible to predict, but I hardly think it will be a big
tragedy. The prime minister maintains that he is open to
discussion with the provinces, all the while making it clear
he expects nothing new from that quarter. . . .' Mr. Bourassa,
in speaking after the Toronto meeting, said that 'the hour
of truth has arrived.' What does that mean, exactly? Does
that mean Quebec will act if Mr. Trudeau acts alone;
will Quebec really take some awesome steps? What kind of
steps? What kind of means? Perhaps we're headed toward

an election on the issue. But would this solve our problems? Even the cleverest constitutions are not universal remedies for our problems."

☐ The *Toronto Globe and Mail* (October 4) criticized Premier Lougheed's stance: "At a time when the country was racked by dissention over wage and price controls and opposition to bilingual programs was hurting, Mr. Trudeau saw fit to introduce in a peremptory way an issue that he could be assured would magnify regional divisions. . . . Thus, the provincial premiers met first in Edmonton and now in Toronto to try and work out a common position with which to approach discussions with Mr. Trudeau. And thus, in both meetings, the country has been treated to the parochial obstinacy of Peter Lougheed who insists on a provincial veto on all constitutional change as the price of his co-operation. To hell with national concerns. To hell with trying to create a sounder framework for a healthy federation. To hell with the needs or aspirations of others. More for Alberta is his slogan. . . . Apologists for Mr. Lougheed can argue that he was only giving back what Alberta has got for far too long. . . . But what kind of a federation can we have when intransigence substitutes for compromise? Regardless of how deep his sense of grievance runs—and with a good deal of justification it must run deep —the rest of us expected more of Mr. Lougheed."

III. QUEBEC AND CANADIAN UNITY

EDITOR'S INTRODUCTION

The grave threat to Canada's unity posed by the animosities between English-speaking and French-speaking Canadians (and centering in the province of Quebec) is the subject of the articles in this section. The situation became even more heated with the November 1976 provincial elections in which separatist Parti Québécois leader René Lévesque won the premiership and his party captured a majority of the seats in Quebec's legislature.

The first selection is an analysis of the unity crisis by Robert Trumbull, a New York *Times* correspondent based in Ottawa. This is followed by an analysis of the "bicultural dimension" of Canadian politics by Dale C. Thomson, vice-principal of Montreal's McGill University.

The next selection is by René Lévesque, who presents his views on the issue of Quebec independence and Canadian unity. And the final article, from *Newsweek* magazine, summarizes the results of Quebec's provincial election and speculates on the future of Quebec and Canada.

THE LANGUAGE DISPUTE AND CANADA'S UNITY [1]

Deep-seated animosities between French-speaking and English-speaking Canadians have plunged their country into a political crisis that, in the view of Prime Minister Pierre Elliott Trudeau and others, threatens to destroy the confederation that has held it together since its founding in 1867.

Differences over language policy, a crucial election issue that has divided Mr. Trudeau's Cabinet and caused antagonism between provinces along ethnic lines, follow a train of

[1] From "Language Dispute Is Termed Threat to Canada's Unity," by Robert Trumbull, staff correspondent based in Ottawa. New York *Times*. p 3. O. 26, '76. © 1976 by The New York Times Company. Reprinted by permission.

periodic confrontations between the two major linguistic groups since French Canada was conquered by Britain more than two centuries ago.

The current outbreak, after a long lull following terrorist incidents in 1970 that shook the country, has been linked to widespread feelings of insecurity caused by inflation and unemployment. Mr. Trudeau, in a recent interview with visiting Japanese correspondents, unpublished in Canada, drew a parallel with a rise in racial tensions in the United States during times of high unemployment.

Many Canadians, including the prime minister, fear that the highly charged exchanges between English and French Canada may lead to the separation of the French-speaking province of Quebec, Canada's largest, with unpredictable effects on the delicate unity of the rest of the nation.

"If certain centrifugal tendencies fulfill themselves," Mr. Trudeau told a meeting of Liberal Party leaders in Toronto . . . [in October 1976], referring to the language crisis and related provincial dissension, "we will have permitted this country either to break up or to become so divided that its existence and its ability to act as one nation will have been destroyed in our time."

Outlook for Quebec Debated

While the strength of the long-standing independence movement in Quebec is debated, as is the economic viability of a separate Quebec state, the seriousness of the rift between the English-speaking majority and the French-speaking minority is accepted across Canada without question. [In the November 1976 provincial elections in Quebec, the separatist Parti Québécois won a majority of seats in the National Assembly and won the premiership for its leader, René Lévesque.—Ed.]

"Terrible hatred seems to be spreading across the nation," Bryce Mackasey, a popular English-speaking [former] federal Cabinet minister from Quebec City, declared in a political speech. . . .

"The French language is suddenly hated for no reason,

[and] French Canadians aren't welcome," said Mr. Mackasey, who . . . resigned as postmaster general in a reported difference with Mr. Trudeau over economic policy.

"We're blessed," he added, referring to the rich heritage of a united Canada, "and we're throwing it away."

The editor of an important western newspaper, in a private conversation, put the odds on keeping Quebec in the confederation at 50-50, noting that the next five years would be crucial.

Willing to "Let French Go"

Judging by such barometers as the popular open-line television shows, street interviews, letters, columns and private exchanges, the inclination among ordinary English-speaking Canadians to "let the French go" is widespread, especially in the west. But not just the west. The outpouring of anti-French sentiment in the letters columns of English-language Toronto newspapers has been frightening, says Claude Ryan, editor of *Le Devoir* a leading French-language newspaper in Montreal.

Among thinking Canadians of both language groups, the anxiety to keep Quebec in the fold is linked to fears that the loss of one province would place a dangerous strain on the tenuous ties with Ottawa in such areas as British Columbia in the west and Nova Scotia in the east, where the gravitational pull of the United States challenges the newer east-west orientation . . . [north] of the border.

Nationalists . . . view the French presence as essential to a distinctive Canadian identity. "Without the French," commented the English-speaking wife of a senior diplomat, also an English-speaking Canadian, "we would be just like the Americans."

Over the generations since the French lost the climactic battle to the British in 1759 on the Plains of Abraham, now a park and tourist attraction in Quebec City, linguistic rivalry has become the focus of other corrosive differences between the two communities.

The wealthy entrepreneurs who might have been planning a diversified economy in French Canada returned to France with the defeated soldiers. The French who remained left their descendants, who now make up about 26 percent of the 22.6 million Canadians, an inherited orientation toward farm, pulpit, academia and the arts, leaving commerce and technology to the English.

In the inevitable drift of youth from farm to city, the bulk of French Canadians sank into the lower occupations. Where the two communities mingled, class distinctions grew. At the same time French Canadians watched with alarm as their culture eroded in the English tide.

Smoldering French Canadian resentment against an inferior lot burst into flame in 1917 and 1942, when young people objected violently to being drafted to fight alongside the British in the two World Wars. The 1942 movement, according to a diary left by William Lyon Mackenzie King, prime minister at the time, had brought Canada to the point of insurrection when the end of World War II defused the crisis.

Subsequently the character of French Canada underwent significant change. A movement in Quebec in the middle 1960's known as the Quiet Revolution swept aside the stultifying grip of the Roman Catholic clergy and opened young French Canadians' eyes to a wider world. Second-class status was no longer good enough.

In 1967 President de Gaulle, after a triumphal motorcade through the heart of French Canada, stood in Montreal and shouted the catch phrase, "Long live Free Quebec!" An outraged Government in Ottawa informed the visitor that he was no longer welcome in Canada, but many French Canadians cheered.

From Irritation to Derision

National emotions were jarred again in 1970 when young French Canadian extremists kidnapped a British diplomat and killed a Quebec cabinet minister in Montreal. Prime Minister Trudeau, in a gesture that is still debated, invoked wartime emergency powers to insure public order.

A year earlier the Trudeau Government had passed the Official Languages Act, guaranteeing that Canadians of either linguistic group could obtain government services on the federal level in their own language. Along with this came a law requiring that all products offered for sale be labeled in both languages and the reclassification of thousands of civil service jobs on a bilingual basis.

The sudden appearance of French on federal road signs and in supermarkets was accepted in areas where French is seldom if ever spoken with feelings ranging from irritation to derision. Businessmen forced to pay for expensive relabeling were not amused, nor were the civil servants who suddenly found themselves studying French, even though the Government paid for the lessons.

The concessions failed to satisfy the French, who still smarted under the continued slights to their language in the predominantly English-speaking provinces. Quebec retaliated with a law making French the sole official language in that province. The English-speaking minority, about 20 percent of the population of six million, was incensed, as were thousands of immigrant parents in Montreal who were informed that they must send their children to French-language schools.

Prime Minister Trudeau, alarmed by an "English backlash," labeled the Quebec legislation stupid.

The English-speaking community was further inflamed by a move to extend the use of French as well as English in air-traffic control towers in Quebec, a step that was postponed for a safety study only after protests by commercial pilots had brought service to a halt for nine days.

QUEBEC AND THE BICULTURAL PROBLEM [2]

Prime Minister [Pierre Elliott] Trudeau once remarked that the real importance of a minority group is not so much

[2] From "Quebec and the Bicultural Dimension," by Dale C. Thomson, vice-principal, McGill University, Montreal. *Academy of Political Science. Proceedings.* v 32, no 2:27-39. '76. Reprinted with permission. Copyright © 1976 by The Academy of Political Science. All rights reserved.

a function of its legal guarantees as its potential to disrupt the country in which it lives. On that basis, French Canada, with the political and administrative apparatus of the province of Quebec behind it, easily qualifies as important.

"Quebec" and "French Canada" are not synonymous terms. Almost 20 percent of the 5.5 million French Canadians live outside that province, and almost 20 percent of Quebec residents are not French Canadians; that is, their first language is not French. But the disruptive power Mr. Trudeau referred to is in the hands of those French Canadians within Quebec. So, for practical purposes, there is a high level of synonymy. And the bicultural dimension of Canada flows from the real power of French Canadians in the province of Quebec.

That is one way of looking at French Canadians—as a minority so troublesome that they might conceivably break up Canada. There are other ways: for instance, as one of the two "founding peoples," a concept utilized by the Royal Commission on Bilingualism and Biculturalism. That concept implies an equal partnership between the descendants of those hardy Frenchmen who first colonized New France and the British who conquered them in 1759. The other Canadians, notably the original settlers, the Indians and Eskimos, and the one-quarter of the Canadian population of origins other than English or French are attributed some lesser status. Those shortcomings acknowledged, the concept of two founding peoples does represent a sincere attempt to transcend psychological divisions that have existed in Canada for more than two centuries and that are still highly pertinent.

The view proffered here of French Canada is more positive than that of a great many, probably most, English Canadians. It challenges the concept of nearly one-third of the total population as a minority to be tolerated only because of some legal guarantees or disruptive potential. French Canada, it posits, is an integral and very important part of Canada, a great asset to be preserved and developed.

The complexities and intracacies of such a pluralist society must be acknowledged. No political leader would choose one if he did have a choice. However, that is the heritage of history.

It is difficult for Americans to realize the full significance of the linguistic dualism of Canada. Many seem to consider it a historical vestige that was illogical to perpetuate and that would disappear with time. There are certainly Canadians who share this view, but it is unlikely to occur soon. Indeed, both the Canadian and Quebec governments are taking steps to see that the opposite occurs.

The Price of Biculturalism

There is undoubtedly a price to be paid for maintaining biculturalism in Canada, and statistics indicate that the highest price is being paid by French Canadians. They are still the second-lowest income group, even in the province of Quebec where they are a majority. Those who speak and write English, particularly those who switch languages, generally do better financially. And yet most French Canadians refer with sadness and even pity to those who have abandoned the language of Molière for that of Shakespeare, or the language of the vast majority of North Americans.

The explanations of this attitude are too complex to deal with here, but it is clear that the great majority of French Canadians feel the loss of their language would be an unacceptable price to pay for the full benefits of the American way of life. At the same time, they are attracted by many of those benefits, both material and nonmaterial. The dilemma facing French Canadians is how to find ways of enjoying the benefits of life in North America while preserving their language.

Until the fairly recent past, material goals did not rank high for French Canadians, or at least for their leaders. In fact, they preserved their language and customs by denying themselves the material benefits that would come from greater integration with the rest of North America. Even during the negotiations that led to the present federal system in Canada, one of the primary goals of French Canadian leaders was to preserve and even strengthen their control over their own way of life. It is too often forgotten, even by English Canadians, that Confederation, in 1867, not only laid the ground work for a country extending from sea to sea but that it put an end to the previous regime, which placed both English and French Canadians under a single government and legislature. This persistence and determination to survive unchanged led Arnold Toynbee to remark that French Canadians would be one of the most durable peoples in human history.

Unfortunately for the French Canadians, the province of Quebec was not rich enough to support their rapidly growing population indefinitely on the basis of a primary economy. Faced in the nineteenth century with a situation described by historian Michel Brunet as "anemic survival," the excess population sought employment in the industrial towns of eastern Canada and New England, and became the urban proletariat working under English language bosses. Their lack of education, knowledge of the language of commerce and industry, and money severely restricted their upward mobility. Of course there was an affluent French Canadian elite, and the poverty level should not be exaggerated, but it cannot be denied that in cities like Montreal economic class and linguistic class cleavages were largely congruent.

Part of the pattern of conduct of French Canadians in Quebec today can be explained as a reaction against that situation. The dam holding this system in place broke as recently as 1959 with the death of Maurice Duplessis, the last provincial premier to stress the traditional nonmaterial values at the expense of economic growth. The arrival in power in Quebec City of the [Jean] Lesage government in June 1960 marked the beginning of a new era of rapid modernization.

At the outset this "quiet revolution," as this modernization process was called, seemed designed primarily to enable Quebec to catch up to more developed parts of Canada, such as the province of Ontario. For this reason many English Canadians welcomed the change of government as likely to bring the objectives of Quebec closer to those of the other provinces and therefore to enhance national unity. However, it soon became evident that there were other ramifications to this process of modernization. It stirred new hope and pride in French-speaking Quebecois, and the Lesage government appealed to that sentiment to pursue its modernizing objectives. For instance, in 1962 it called an election to strengthen its position and campaigned in favor of nationalization of the electrical power companies in the province. Its slogan, which proved eminently successful, was *maîtres chez nous* or "masters in our own house." Lesage also carried on and intensified the struggle with Ottawa for a larger share of taxing powers and other financial resources. He surprised the rest of Canada even more, particularly since he was a former federal cabinet minister, by demanding increased legislative autonomy for Quebec as well. In 1964, Canadians witnessed a spectacle—certainly unanticipated by either man a few years earlier when they were members of the St. Laurent cabinet in Ottawa—of Prime Minister [Lester] Pearson and Premier Lesage playing brinkmanship with Confederation in their dispute over control of social welfare legislation.

The quiet revolution of the 1960s in Quebec must be seen in the context of worldwide events and conditions. As British Prime Minister Harold Macmillan said at the time, "winds of change" were sweeping the continents. Its defenses already being eroded by industrialization, improved communications, and other factors, Quebec was no longer immune to these currents. For instance, news of national liberation movements in Asia and Africa struck a responsive chord among French Canadians and stimulated the centuries-old dream of wiping out the British conquest. After years of acquiescence, separatist movements appeared once more, and public opinion polls in 1963 indicated that 13 percent of Quebecois openly favored independence. Acts of terrorism were committed by some extreme separatist groups that included at least one person who had had experience in Algeria and another in the Congo. The most infamous of these was the kidnapping in October 1970 of British diplomat James Cross and of Quebec Labour Minister Pierre Laporte. The latter was assassinated. It is significant as an indication of the state of public opinion in Quebec at the time that while many people thought the kidnapping of the British diplomat a good trick to play on *les Anglais,* the vast majority of French Canadians were horrified at the assassination of Laporte and approved the firm action of the Canadian and Quebec governments to restore order. Many expressed deep concern that foreigners, hearing perhaps of Quebec for the first time, would get a wrong impression of it.

Renewing Links With France

Another facet of the quiet revolution was the renewal of links with France and the development of new links with other French-speaking peoples. French-speaking Quebecois have always had difficulty in accepting the Canadian government in Ottawa as "their" government, and that was probably a factor in the decision of the Quebec government to establish direct working relations with France rather than going through Ottawa. It must be pointed out that these relationships were restricted to fields of provincial jurisdiction, but at the same time they fell within the ambit of any reasonable definition of "foreign affairs" and consequently were of direct interest to the federal government. President de Gaulle, encouraged by a small group of politicians and officials in France, many of whom saw an analogy with contemporary events in French-speaking Africa, encouraged these direct contacts. By 1967, he had apparently become convinced that the independence of Quebec was inevitable, and he took the opportunity of his visit to Expo in Montreal in July of that year to *poser un geste* (make a gesture) in its favor. His adoption of the separatist cry, *Vive le Québec libre,* shouted from the balcony of the Montreal Hôtel de Ville, echoed around the world. He certainly did succeed in encouraging the separatists. On the other hand, he stirred the Canadian national sentiments of many millions of Canadians, both English- and French-speaking, and spurred the federal government to defend its prerogatives. Its first act was to declare his intervention in Canadian affairs "unacceptable" and force him to return to France the next day.

Since that time, thanks in part to changes in leadership in Paris, Ottawa, and Quebec City, a new *modus vivendi* has been reached, according to which Ottawa's overriding authority in international matters is recognized, but Quebec does have considerable interaction with other countries, including France, and the Quebec government has a special voice through participation in Canadian delegations when its interests are involved. The extent of Quebec's external relations astonishes some theorists of federalism, but they do reflect the ability of the Canadian federal system to adapt to political realities. To sum up on this point, it is fair to say that relations between France and Canada are once again normal, but the "normality" is rather different from the *status quo ante.* Each year thousands of Frenchmen and Quebecois cross the Atlantic under a variety of cooperative arrangements. Will these relations tend to weaken Quebec's ties with Canada and the rest of North America? There is a possibility, but there is also evidence that better knowledge of France and the French has led Quebecois to realize how very North American they are.

Recent Changes in Quebec

But the real measure of the quiet revolution and its long-range significance must be taken within Quebec and based on both material and nonmaterial changes. The Lesage government was defeated in 1966, but the Union Nationale party, which governed from 1966 to 1970, and the . . . Liberal administration under Robert Bourassa, a former lieutenant of Lesage, . . . carried the province forward along the same path. [In the November 1976 elections in Quebec, the separatist Parti Québécois candidate for premier, René Lévesque, defeated Bourassa and the party won a majority of seats in Quebec's legislature.—Ed.] Quebec is now a highly industrialized province, with agriculture accounting for only 9 percent of production. A radically new system of education has been established, replacing the former highly elitist, church-sponsored one, which had been designed essentially to train priests and members of the liberal professions. Quebec now has a comprehensive system of social welfare, including Medicare. Regional-economic development programs have greatly increased revenues in the poorer outlying regions, and the public service has grown rapidly.

More difficult to evaluate are the present norms, values, and attitudes of Quebecois. What, for instance, is their attitude toward the long-standing preoccupation with their survival as a group? Has this sentiment diminished? The evidence is contradictory. On one hand, qualified young Quebecois are not hesitant about demanding their place in the sun. They display a confidence that certainly seems new. On the other hand, there is no doubt that their society is more vulnerable to outside influences than ever before.

Politicians apparently still feel that the sentiment of insecurity is a factor to be reckoned with and do not hesitate to prey on it. René Lévesque, the leader of the separatist party, the Parti Québécois, declares at regular intervals that if independence is not achieved within ten years, no one will have the right to speak French in Quebec. And even [former] Premier Bourassa . . . [evoked] it in support of his policies to strengthen the position of French by government action. Some might see in the growing popularity of the separatist movement an indication of continuing insecurity. Others interpret that phenomenon as a growth of self-confidence, a feeling that French Canadians in Quebec have reached a level of development where they can take charge completely of their own affairs and run their own country. The issue of separatism today no longer seems as emotional and as abstract as a decade ago, when it was often characterized by an outpouring of frustration and nourished by privation and inequality. Today, the possibility of separation is just another, though very serious, option in Quebec.

A related question is whether, having achieved a fair degree of modernization and competence, with greater opportunities for careers within the province of Quebec, French Canadians' attitudes toward Ottawa have changed. It is fortunate from the point of view of those who believe in a single Canada that throughout most of the period since 1960 its government has been in the hands of people able to understand this process of modernization and willing to support it. If the situation that pertained there in the 1950s still existed, when the working language of the federal public service was almost exclusively English and French was not allowed on public signs in the city of Ottawa, there is little doubt that modern day young French Canadians would be inclined to turn their backs on it.

Fortunately, the Pearson government and its successor, the Trudeau government, have taken significant initiatives, one of the first of which was the creation of the Royal Commission on Bilingualism and Biculturalism, set up in 1963, with Dr. Davidson Dunton as one of the two co-chairmen. That massive investigation resulted, among other things, in both English and French being made official languages within the areas of jurisdiction of the federal government. Associated steps, such as enabling citizens to be served by the federal public service in either language and enabling young French-speaking Canadians to be on a comparable footing when starting their careers in Ottawa, have had a salutary effect. In the Department of External Affairs, for example, a high level of bilingualism has been achieved, that is, officials are bilingual and may work in either language. In the circumstances and since much of the work that the federal government offers is more challenging than that in Quebec, some of the resistance to making a career in Ottawa has been overcome. The increasing self-confidence of young French Canadians has also had the effect of making them more inclined to accept the challenge of the federal public service.

Other types of measures must also be borne in mind, such as the regional economic development program, through which vast sums of money were poured into rural areas of Quebec. Another example is the system of equalization payments, through which taxes raised by the federal government are redistributed to the provinces in such a way that they can all provide a similar level of provincial services. Quebec is a very important beneficiary of this system. Generally speaking, the policy of the federal government has been to induce Quebecois to identify more with the rest of Canada, particularly with the national capital, and to perceive the advantages of remaining a part of Canada.

These policies have been pursued in the face of a substantial backlash, particularly in the western provinces, against the more visible French presence in Ottawa, the demands of Quebec, and the cost of programs such as bilingualization and federal payments that end up in Quebec. It is not easy to weigh the threat to Canada from Quebec separatism against the hostility of some other parts of Canada to measures designed to meet that threat. And in periods of economic austerity, the federal government's position is more difficult still.

The Federal Government and Quebec

A sobering thought for the federal government in determining its policies to meet the problem of Quebec and biculturalism is that there is no complete solution. Most of Canada will remain essentially "English" and, at best, Ottawa will be only half-French. By and large, French Canadians will continue to feel more at home in Quebec than elsewhere in Canada. Hence their first loyalty will be to Quebec, in contrast to residents of the other provinces, whose first loyalty is quite clearly to Canada as a whole. Other, more international, forces will also contribute to the outcome, such as future economic conditions, the future course of nationalism, regional regroupings, and world peace in general.

When the Liberal government of Robert Bourassa was elected in Quebec in 1970 on an unabashedly profederal ticket, there was widespread hope that he and Pierre Trudeau would work closely together to keep Quebec happy within Confederation. However, in many instances, the two governments . . . appeared to be at odds, even in their language policies. Bourassa first won election on the slogan of "profitable federalism," a somewhat cynical claim that he and his party could extract more money from Ottawa than anyone else. He was appealing to a majority sentiment in Quebec, carefully ascertained in advance by polls, that the primary concerns of the voters were material in nature and that these could best be solved within Confederation. In this vein, he promised to create 100,000 additional jobs in a short period. Because he was elected with such a clear commitment to federalism, many Canadians expected him to cooperate fully in the process of constitutional review then under way but long delayed because of Quebec's particular demands. However, when the crunch came following the constitutional conference in Victoria, British Columbia, in 1971, he found a pretext at the last moment to avoid placing the constitutional revisions before the Quebec legislature, and so the efforts of several years came to naught. He gained some political credit within Quebec for "standing up" to Ottawa. Whether or not he did Canada a great disservice in the long run will be deterinmed by history.

As they prepared for new elections in 1973, Bourassa and his colleagues decided to add another dimension to their program and adopted the further slogan, "cultural sovereignty." It was clearly designed to undercut the Parti Québécois, the separatist party, and clearly the principal threat to the Liberals. Through this tandem of "profitable federalism" and "cultural sovereignty," Bourassa was borrowing at least the words of the first program devised by separatist leader René Lévesque, "sovereignty-association," or sovereignty of Quebec in association, presumably economic and financial, with the rest of Canada. Looked at another way, Bourassa was telling the Quebec electorate it could have the material advantages of Confederation and yet remain French. The appeal was not unlike that made by George-Etienne Cartier in selling Confederation to Quebecois in 1867. The strategy worked: the Liberals were returned with a fantastic majority of 102 out of 110 seats. However, the Parti Québécois, the separatist party, increased its popular vote to between 32 and 33 percent, but because of the single constituency system won only six seats.

The 1973 elections marked the clear polarization of the Quebec electorate, with separatism as the clear alternative to Bourassa-type federalism. . . .

Bourassa's first major step in implementing his policy of cultural sovereignty was to rush through the legislature in the summer of 1974 a bill making French the official language of Quebec. The expression "priority language" would be more appropriate, since English still retains an important but reduced role. But for a man with Bourassa's keen political instincts, the word "official," even if less accurate, had greater value. In brief, the Official Language Act, or Bill 22, as it is commonly called, aims to make it possible for Quebecois to use French in their province, while respecting the rights of the English-language population to their educational system. The "English" may also use English in many other instances, but overall the official language is French. In the field of business, firms must undertake "francization" programs and open up as many jobs as possible to French-speaking persons. Provision is made for all French-speaking children to learn English as a second language, and vice versa; but it will be many years before the school system is able to carry out the terms of that provision.

Thus, while Ottawa has been moving to promote bilingualism, the Quebec government has moved toward greater unilingualism. Is this a case of the two governments working at cross-purposes? Perhaps to some degree. On the other hand, it can well be argued that the future of bilingualism in Canada depends on the viability of French in Quebec. If it is not made "secure" there, and here again is the historic French Canadian preoccupation with security, attempts to promote it elsewhere in Canada will be of no avail. One can also argue that if Quebec separates, then attempts to encourage bilingualism in the rest of Canada will certainly be futile. And one must recognize clearly that the language law is designed to reduce the appeal of separatism. From those points of view, then, the provincial and federal language acts are complementary and mutually supporting.

The Official Language Act

At the time it was passed, the Official Language Act raised a storm of protests, particularly from what Bourassa called both English and French extremists, that is, those who felt it repressed the English and those who felt it did not do so enough. Many in between were also unhappy about aspects of this legislation, either on the grounds of principle, common sense, or practicality. However, they had to recognize that Premier Bourassa had again pulled a political trump card out of his sleeve. Polls taken a few months after the law was passed indicated that he had succeeded in defusing the language issue among young French Canadians. By coincidence or not, the percentage of separatists among junior college students fell from about 80 to about 50 percent. The Parti Québécois continues to attack the legislation as mere "tokenism," but it is the English-language population that has protested the most as it has been applied. . . .

At the beginning of the 1975–76 school year, a furor was caused in the Montreal area when children were obliged for the first time, in accordance with the new law, to take a language test to enter an English-language school. Some

Italian immigrant children passed the tests but were not enrolled because the law also sets a quota for every school district, based on past enrollments. An English-language Montreal radio station seized on the issue and campaigned to have the law repealed. Bourassa met the enraged citizens in a public confrontation, stood firm—thereby improving his image among the French-speaking citizenry—and then set to work quietly to find a practical way of allowing the some 200 children who had been excluded by the quota system to attend an English-language school. The premier's performance was not quite perfect: his minister of education, who had been growing increasingly unhappy with his place in the cabinet, resigned on the grounds that no such concession should be made and that the possibility of attending an English-language school should be restricted to children of proven English homes. Bourassa had no difficulty in finding another minister of education.

What are the likely long-term consequences of this language law? If [former] Premier Bourassa and his colleagues had their choice, they would apply it gradually over a long period of time and moderate its provisions with large doses of common sense and realism. Because their aim was to remove the language issue from political debates, or at least to formulate the debate in terms favorable to them, they . . . [were] anxious to have as few eruptions as possible in its application. It is hoped that a majority of Quebecois, both English- and French-speaking, will recognize that the legislation is about as good as can be devised at the moment and will put it to the test of practice. A great deal of flexibility and discretion is provided for, and one can be confident that the government will use them to reconcile divergent interests and views. . . .

Thus a new pattern of bilingualism appears to be emerging in Canada, one that can be called *quid pro quo* bilingualism: as many rights for the English in Quebec as are accorded to the French in the other provinces and as much linguistic equality as possible in the national capital. Un-

doubtedly it will be difficult for the federal government to
go further, or to encourage the other provinces to go further,
in extending bilingualism throughout the other nine provinces. The backlash was strong before the Quebec law was
passed; it has grown stronger since. However, there is real
hope that progress can be made in improving the bilingual
character of the national capital.

This trend suggests that Canada is moving away from
the concept once advanced of integral bilingualism throughout the federation, with everyone having some knowledge of
both languages. It will probably not even be possible to attain that goal within the federal public service, particularly
outside of Ottawa. It is not a comparison that is appealing,
but perhaps Canada is getting nearer to the Belgian model
with two unilingual areas and a bilingual capital. Of course,
come what may, whether they separate, partially separate, or
whatever, French-speaking Quebecois will have a greater
need to know English than the majority of English-speaking
Canadians in other provinces will have to learn French.

One of the likely consequences of this linguistic legislation, combined with new arrangements between Quebec and
Ottawa to discourage immigration to Quebec of persons
who are not prepared to make French their principal language, is that Quebec will fall behind other parts of Canada
in population and economic growth. By 1985, Quebec will
be short of manpower, and neither immigration nor natural
population increase seem likely to fill the gap. (One aspect
of Quebec's modernization is that its birthrate has fallen to
the lowest in Canada.) There is a good chance that capital
will not be as easily attracted to Quebec as to other parts
of Canada, and this will increase the disparity in economic
importance between Quebec and, say, Ontario. It is fairly
safe to forecast that by the year 2000 Ontario will be at least
twice as large as Quebec in terms of population and that
Toronto rather than Montreal will be the financial capital
of Canada. Quebec will constitute only about 20 percent
of the population of Canada, and its representation in the

Canadian Parliament will have to be adjusted accordingly. This last factor will again stimulate Quebecois' feeling of insecurity within Canada and may fuel separatism.

Social Change in Quebec

But those are rather long-term predictions. The question is whether the two sets of language legislation, Quebec and federal, and other actions will get Canada through another generation. Perhaps it would not be too optimistic to say they will. Much is made of the radical changes in Quebec since 1960, and particularly in the attitudes of French Canadians. Graphic illustrations are put forward of the decline in respect for authority, both of the church and of the state. Attention is drawn to the marked decrease in church attendance, the widespread use of the birth control pill, the frequency of abortions, the rising crime rate, and the numerous illegal strikes.

It is quite true that there has been a radical departure from past social patterns. And yet it can be argued that the new patterns only appear radical in today's world in comparison with the former traditional Quebec society. Compared to those of the youth of many other parts of the world, including English Canada and the United States, the attitudes and conduct of young French Canadians are relatively moderate. It must be remembered that the youth of today in Quebec are still the first generation to be "liberated" from the old constraints and are perhaps pursuing the enjoyment of that new liberty rather far, but that is a situation that will certainly correct itself with time.

For instance, there is concern with the low birthrate in Quebec, yet polls indicate that a high value is still placed on the family and on children. Almost certainly the birthrate will rise again, but childbearing will occur a few years later in a woman's life. In other words, the trend is not against the family unit and childbearing but in favor of a more relaxed, voluntaristic type of marital relationship and family planning, such as has become widespread in other parts of North America in the recent past. Similarly, with regard to public authority, or law and order, reference has already been made to the strong public reaction against the terrorist excesses in 1970. The same attitude was quite evident in the fall of 1975 in the case of strikes in the public service, including the post office and urban transport systems. In earlier days, resisting public authority was a way of thumbing one's nose at *les Anglais;* today, it represents a conflict between French Canadians.

Since World War II, it has been learned time and again that change breeds stress, and that progress is only accomplished at the price of some measure of conflict. Quebec is still engaged in a sweeping process of change and progress. It is far from having run its course. On balance, the results so far have been positive. Hence there is reason to be optimistic about the future. Fate has not been kind to French Canadians, making them a small linguistic minority on this continent; they merit understanding and even support in their legitimate goals, which are not essentially different from those of any other people.

Quebec and Canadian-American Relations

Finally . . . , it must be asked what the state of Quebec and of the bicultural dimension of Canada means in terms of Canada-United States relations. Assuming first that Quebec will not separate from the rest of Canada, there are no major implications. The increased French Canadian input into Canadian decision making is scarcely likely to strengthen anti-American trends. Because they have the protective barrier of a different language, French Canadians feel less threatened by American influences and in a better position to take or leave what the United States has to offer. In other words, anti-American sentiment is much stronger in Toronto than it is in Quebec City. Ottawa's Foreign Investment Review Act resulted from pressures in English Canada and has not been received with enthusiasm by the government of Quebec, which is still trying to attract capital from south of the border for development projects. [The act places several restrictions on the kinds and amounts of foreign investment allowed in Canada. The act, however, is not strictly enforced.—Ed.]

American firms operating in Quebec will, of course, be expected to obey the Official Language Act, which means essentially opening up positions to French Canadians and giving them the opportunity to work in French. The day is gone when the American head of a big firm could say, as happened as recently as 1972, that as long as he was president no French would be used in the Montreal headquarters. Incidentally, he is no longer head of that firm. On the other hand, one cannot imagine the government of Quebec applying so much pressure on an American firm to "francize" its operations that it will withdraw from the province. Persuasion, not coercion, is the order of the day. Generally speaking, American firms will be expected to see that their interests lie in adhering to the objectives of the Official Language Act. Past experience in other countries suggests that they will do so. Quebec officials are likely to continue to be happy to deal with Americans in English, whether in Quebec or across the border. It is the English Canadians whom they want to force to use French!

Nor is the bilingualization of the federal public service likely to make much difference in the field of Canada-United States relations. In recent years, a French Canadian served as ambassador to Washington. He was able by his presence to draw attention to the fact that part of the population of Canada is French-speaking. He was also inclined to stand somewhat more on protocol than his immediate predecessor, and his *cuisine* was true *cordon bleu!* But it is doubtful that Americans he dealt with noticed many more significant differences. Certainly his concept of Canada was all-Canadian. Other French Canadians in the Canadian public service could not be expected to act differently. . . .

It would be better to conclude by saying that the recent evolution of Quebec and the growing bicultural dimension of Canada have had positive effects on Canada-United States relations. The modernization of Quebec has improved its capacity to contribute to the well-being of the whole continent. The assertion of the "French fact" in Canada has increased awareness of the distinctiveness of Canada from the United States, and a greater realization of this distinctiveness by American negotiators could make relations easier. Canadian negotiators have long complained that their American counterparts were not sensitive to such domestic factors. Finally, the total effect has been to strengthen Canada as a nation and as a partner of the United States on this continent.

FOR AN INDEPENDENT QUEBEC [3]

What does Québec want? The question is an old cliché in Canadian political folklore. Again and again, during the more than 30 years since the end of World War II, it's been raised whenever Québec's attitudes made it the odd man out in the permanent pull and tug of our federal-provincial relations. In fact, it's a question which could go back to the British conquest of an obscure French colony some 15 years before American Independence, and then run right through the stubborn survival of those 70,000 settlers and their descendants during the following two centuries.

By now there are some six million of them in Canada, not counting the progeny of the many thousands who were forced by poverty, especially around the turn of the century, to migrate to the United States, and now constitute substantial "Franco" communities in practically all the New England states.

But Québec remains the homeland. All along the valley of the St. Lawrence, from the Ottawa River down to the Gaspé peninsula and the great Gulf [of St. Lawrence], in the

[3] From "For an Independent Québec," by René Lévesque, cofounder of the Mouvement Souveraineté-Association, and of the Parti Québécois in 1967-68 of which he is now president. *Foreign Affairs.* 54:734-44. Jl. '76. Reprinted by permission from *Foreign Affairs*, July 1976. Copyright 1976 by Council on Foreign Relations, Inc.

ancient settlements which grew into the big cities of Montréal and Québec, in hundreds of smaller towns and villages from the American border to the mining centers and power projects in the north, there are now some 4.8 million "Québécois." That's 81 percent of the population of the largest and second most populous of Canada's ten provinces.

What does this French Québec want? Sometime during the next few years, the question may be answered. And there are growing possibilities that the answer could very well be—independence.

Launched in 1967-68, the Parti Québécois . . . [has a platform] based on political sovereignty. . . . In its first electoral test in 1970, it already had had 24 percent of the votes. Then in 1973, a second general election saw it jump to 30 percent, and, although getting only six out of 110 seats, become what our British-type parliamentary system calls the Official Opposition, i.e., the government's main interlocutor and challenger. [The November 1976 provincial elections in Québec saw the election of Lévesque as premier and his party win a majority of the seats in the National Assembly.—Ed.] . . .

The Rise of the Province Before World War II

There was the definite outline of a nation in that small French colony which was taken over, in 1763, by the British Empire at its apogee. For over a century and a half, beginning just before the Pilgrim Fathers landed in the Boston area, that curious mixture of peasants and adventurers had been writing a proud history all over the continent. From Hudson Bay to the Gulf of Mexico, and from Labrador to the Rockies, they had been the discoverers, the fur-traders, the fort-builders. Out of this far-ranging saga, historically brief though it was, and the tenacious roots which at the same time were being sunk into the St. Lawrence lowlands, there slowly developed an identity quite different from the original stock as well as from France of the *ancien régime;* just as different, in its way, as the American identity had become from its own British seeds. Thus, when the traumatic shock of the conquest happened, it had enough staying power to survive, tightly knit around its Catholic clergy and its country landowners.

Throughout the next hundred years, while English Canada was being built, slowly but surely, out of the leftovers of the American Revolution and as a rampart against America's attacks of Manifest Destiny, French Québec managed to hang on—mostly because of its "revenge of the cradles." It was desperately poor, cut off from the decision-making centers both at home and in Great Britain, and deprived of any cultural nourishment from its former mother country. But its rural, frugal society remained incredibly prolific. So it grew impressively, at least in numbers. And it held on obstinately, according to its lights and as much as its humble means made it possible, to those two major ingredients of national identity—land and language. The hold on land was at best tenuous and, as in any colonial context, confined to the multitude of small farm holdings. Everything else—from the growth of major cities to the setting-up of manufacturing industries and then the rush of resource development—was the exclusive and undisputed field of action of "les Anglais," the growing minority of Anglo-Saxon and then-assimilated immigrant groups who ran most of Québec under the compact leadership of Montreal-based entrepreneurs, financiers and merchant kings.

As for the French elite, it remained mostly made up of doctors, lawyers, and priests—"essential services" for the bodies and souls of cheap labor, whose miraculous birthrate kept the supply continuously overabundant. And naturally, there were politicians, practically all of that typical colonial breed which is tolerated as long as it keeps natives happily excited about accessories and divided on essentials.

Needless to say, the educational system was made both to reflect this type of society and to keep it going nicely and quietly. There was a modest collection of church-run seminaries, where the main accent was on recruiting for the priesthood, and which, for over a century, led to just one underdeveloped university. For nine-tenths of the children, there was nothing but grammar school, if that. Read and write barely enough to sign your name, and then, without any time for "getting ideas," graduate to obedient respectful employment by any boss generous enough to offer a steady modest job.

Such was the culturally starved and economically inferior, but well-insulated and thus highly resistant, French Québec which, 109 years ago, was lead into the final mutation of British North America and its supreme defense against American expansionism: Confederation, of four eastern colonies as a beginning, but soon to run north of the border "from sea to sea." Into that impressive Dominion, originally as one of four and eventually one of ten provinces, Québec was incorporated without trouble and generally without enthusiasm. From now on, it was to be a minority forever, and, with the help of a dynamic federal immigration policy, a steadily diminishing one. In due time, it would probably merge and disappear into the mainstream, or at the most remain as a relatively insignificant and yet convenient ghetto: *la différence*.

As the building of Canada accelerated during the late nineteenth and early twentieth centuries, a tradition was established that Québec was to get its measured share of the work, anytime there was enough to go around—and the same for rewards. And so, in a nutshell, it went until fairly recently. All told, it hasn't been such a bad deal, this status of "inner colony" in a country owned and managed by another national entity. Undoubtedly, French Québec was (as it remains to this day) the least ill-treated of all colonies in the world. Under a highly centralized federal system, which is much closer to a unitary regime than American federalism, it was allowed its full panoply of provincial institutions: cabinet, legislature, courts, along with the quasi-permanent fun of great squabbles, usually leading to exciting election campaigns, about the defense or extension of its "state rights"! On three occasions during the last 80 years, one of "its own" has even been called upon—at times when there was felt a particular need to keep the natives quiet—to fill the most flattering of all offices, that of federal prime minister. Last but not least of the three, Mr. [Pierre Elliott] Trudeau, of whose "Canadian nationalism" it is naturally part and parcel, did as splendidly as was humanly possible for most of the last ten years in this big-chief-of Québec dimension of the job. But the law of diminishing returns, along with the inevitable way of all (including political) flesh, has been catching up with his so-called French Power in Ottawa. And no replacement seems to be in sight.

New Nationalism

But this is getting ahead of our story. To understand the rise of Québec's own new nationalism and its unprecedented drive toward self-government, we must go back at least as far as World War II. Not that the dream had completely vanished during the two long centuries of survival which have just been described—from an admittedly partisan, but, I honestly believe, not unfair viewpoint. In the 1830s, for instance, there even was an ill-advised and disastrous armed rebellion by a few hundred "Patriots," leading to bloody repression and lasting memories about what not to do. And it is rather significant, by the way, that it took until just now before the poor heroic victims of that abortive rebellion became truly rehabilitated in popular opinion.

Small and impotent though it was, and in spite of feeling that this condition would possibly last forever, French Québec never quite forgot the potential nation it had once been, never quite gave up dreaming about some miracle which might bring back its chance in the future. In some distant, indescribable future. Now and then, there were stirrings: a writer here, a small political coterie there; a great upsurge of nationalist emotions, in the 1880s, around the Riel affair—the hanging by "les Anglais" of the French-speaking leader of the Prairie Métis; then in 1917, on the conscription issue, a bitter and frequently violent confrontation between the Empire-minded English and the "isolationist" French; faint stirrings again in the Twenties; stronger ones in the Thirties.

Then World War II, with a repeat, in 1944, of the total disagreement on conscription. But mostly, here as elsewhere, this most terrible of all wars was also a midwife for revolutionary change. Thankfully in less disruptive a manner than in other parts of the world, it did start a revolution in Québec. Wartime service, both overseas and on the industrial home-front, dealt a mortal blow to the old order, gave an irresistible impetus to urbanization and started the breakup of the traditional rural-parish ideal, yanked women by the thousands into war-plant industry and as many men into battle-dress discovery of the great wide world. For a small cooped-up society, this was a more traumatic experience than for most others. And then when the post war years brought the Roaring Fifties, unprecedented mobility, and television along with a consumer society, the revolution had to become permanent.

The beginning of the 1960s saw it baptized officially: the Quiet Revolution, with the adjective implying that "quaint old Québec" couldn't have changed all that much. But it had. Its old set of values literally shattered, it was feeling collectively naked, like a lobster during its shedding season, looking frantically about for a new armor with which to face the modern world. The first and most obvious move was toward education. After so prolonged and scandalous a neglect of this most basic instrument of development, it was quickly realized that here was the first urgent bootstrap operation that had to be launched. It was done with a vengeance: from one of the lowest in the Western world, Québec per capita investment in education rapidly became, and remains, one of the very highest. Not always well spent (but who is to throw the first stone?), with many mistakes along the way, and the job still far from complete, which it will never be anyway; but the essential results are there, and multiplying: human resources that are, at long last, getting required development, along with a somewhat equal chance for all and a normal furious rise in general expectations. The same, naturally, is happening also in other fields, quite particularly in that of economics, the very first where such rising expectations were bound to strike against the wall of an entrenched colonial setup, with its now intolerable second-class status for the French majority, and the stifling remote control of nearly all major decisions either in Ottawa or in alien corporate offices.

Inevitably, there had to be a spillover into politics. More than half of our public revenue and most of the decisions that count were and are in outside hands, in a federal establishment which was basically instituted not by or for us, but by others and, always first and foremost, for their own purposes. With the highly centralized financial system that this establishment constitutionally lords over, this means, for example, that about 80 percent of Québec savings and potential investment capital ends up in banks and insurance companies whose operations are none of our business. It also means, just for example once again, that immigration is also practically none of our business; and this could have, and is having, murderous effects on a minority people with a birthrate, changed like everything else in less than a generation, down from its former prodigious level to close to zero population growth.

Throughout the 1960s, these and other problems were interminably argued about and batted back and forth between federal politicians and bureaucrats ("What we have we hold, until we get more") and a succession of insistent but orthodox, no more than rock-the-boat, nationalists in Québec. But while this dialogue of the deaf was going on and on, the idea of political independence reappeared as it had to. Not as a dream this time, but as a project, and very quickly as a serious one. This developed by leaps and bounds from easily ridiculed marginal groups to small semi-organized political factions, and finally to a full-fledged na-

tionalist party in 1967–68. These were the same two years
during which, by pure coincidence, Mr. Trudeau was just
as rapidly being elevated to the heights as a new federalist
champion from Québec.

But in spite of his best efforts and those of his party's
branch-plant in provincial government, and through an un-
ceasing barrage of money, vilification and rather repugnant
fear-inducing propaganda, the voters have democratically
brought the Parti Québécois . . . to power. Which brings us
right back to our starting-point. . . .

What Does the Province Want?

. . . The way we see it, it would have to go somewhat like
this. There is a new Québec government which is totally
dedicated to political independence. But this same Québec,
for the time being, is still very much a component of federal
Canada, with its quite legitimate body of elected representatives in Ottawa. This calls, first of all, for at least a try at
negotiation. But fruitful talk between two equally legitimate
and diametrically opposed levels of government, without
any further pressure from the population—that would be a
real first in Canadian political history! Obviously, there
would have to be the referendum which the Parti Québécois
proposes in order to get the decisive yes-or-no answer to
the tired question: What *does* Québec want? (This was
precisely the procedure by which the only new province to
join Confederation during our recent democratic past, Newfoundland, was consulted in 1948–49 about whether or not
to opt in. So why not about opting out?) If the answer
should be no, then there's nothing to do but wait for the
momentum of change to keep on working until we all find
out whether or not there is finally to be a nation here. If
the answer is yes, out, then the pressure is on Ottawa, along
with a rather dramatic surge of outside attention, and we
all get a privileged opportunity to study the recently inked
Helsinki Declaration and other noble documents about self-
determination for all peoples.

Fully confident of the basic integrity of Canadian democracy, and just as conscious that any silliness would be very costly for both sides, we firmly believe that the matter would then be brought to a negotiated settlement. Especially since the Parti Québécois, far from aiming at any kind of mutual hostility or absurd Berlin Wall, will then repeat its standing offer of a new kind of association, as soon as it is agreed to get rid of our illusion of deep unshakeable national unity, when in fact here are two quite real and distinct entities in an obsolete and increasingly morbid majority/minority relationship. Our aim is simply full equality by the only means through which a smaller nation can reasonably expect to achieve it with a larger one: self-government. But we are definitely not unaware of the shock waves that such a break, after so long an illusion of eternity, is bound to send through the Canadian political fabric.

We do not accept the simplistic domino theory, where Québec's departure is presented as the beginning of fatal dislocation, with "separatism" spreading in all directions like a galloping disease until the balkanized bits and pieces are swallowed up by the huge maw next door. In spite of the somewhat unsure character of its national identity and its excessive satellization by the American economic and cultural empire, Canada-without-Québec has enough "différence" left, sufficient traditions and institutional originality, to withstand the extraction of its "foreign body" and find a way to go on from there. It might even turn out to be a heaven-sent opportunity to revamp the overcentralized and ridiculously bureaucratized federal system, that century-old sacred cow which, for the moment, nobody dares to touch seriously for fear of encouraging Québec's subversive leanings!

Be that as it may, we know there would be a traumatic moment and a delicate transition during which things might go wrong between us for quite a while, or else, one would hope, start going right as never before. With this strange new-colored Québec on the map between Ontario and the Maritime provinces [Nova Scotia, New Brunswick, and

Prince Edward Island], Canada must be kept from feeling incurably "Pakistanized," so we must address ourselves without delay to the problem of keeping a land bridge open with as much free flow of people and goods as is humanly possible; as much and more as there is, I would imagine, between Alaska and the main body of the United States over the western land bridge.

Such a scenario would call, as a decisive first step, for a customs union, as full-fledged as both countries consider to be mutually advantageous. We have, in fact, been proposing that ever since the Parti Québécois was founded, and naturally meeting with the most resonant silence in all orthodox federalist circles. But in the midst of that silence, not a single responsible politician, nor for that matter a single important businessman, has been heard to declare that it wouldn't happen if and when the time comes. For indisputably such a partnership, carefully negotiated on the basis of equality, is bound to be in the cards. Nothing prevents one envisaging it, for instance, going immediately, or at least very quickly, as far as the kind of monetary union which the European Common Market, with its original six and now nine members, has been fitfully aiming at for so many years. And building on this foundation, it would lead this new "northern tier" to a future immeasurably richer and more stimulating than the 109-year-old bind in which two nations more often than not feel and act like Churchill's two scorpions in the same bottle.

A "National" Future?

What of Québec's own national future, both internal and international, in this context of sovereignty-cum-interdependence?

The answers here, for reasons that are evident, have to be brief, even sketchy and essentially tentative. The perspective of nationhood, for people who haven't been there yet, is bound to be an uncertain horizon. The more so in a period of history like ours, when so much is changing so fast you get the feeling that maybe change itself is becoming the only law to be counted on. Who can pretend to know exactly what or where his country will be 25 or even just ten years from now?

One thing sure, is that Québec will not end up, either soon or in any foreseeable future, as the anarchic caricature of a revolutionary banana republic which adverse propaganda has been having great sinister fun depicting in advance. Either-Ottawa-or is very simply inspired by prejudice, the origin of this nonsense mostly to be found in the tragic month of October 1970 and the great "crisis" which our political establishments, under the astutely calculating Mr. Trudeau, managed to make out of a couple of dozen young terrorists, whose ideology was a hopeless hodgepodge of anarcho-nationalism and kindergarten Marxism, which had no chance of having any kind of serious impact. What they *did* accomplish was two kidnappings and, most cynically welcome of all, one murder—highly unfortunate but then also particularly par for the course in the international climate at the time. What was not par at all, however, was the incredible abuse of power for which those events, relatively minor per se, were used as a pretext: the careful buildup of public hysteria, army trucks rolling in during the night, and then, for months on end, the application in Québec, and solely in Québec, of a federal War Measures Act for which no peacetime precedent exists in any democratic country. A great spectacle produced in order to terrorize the Québécois forever back into unquestioning submissiveness, and, outside, to feed the mill of scary propaganda about how dangerous this tame animal could nevertheless be!

In actual fact, French Québec, with its normal share of troubles, disquiet and, now, the same kind of social turmoil and search for new values that are rampant all over the Western world, remains at bottom a very solid, well-knit and nonviolent society. Even its new and demanding nationalism has about itself something less strident and essentially more self-confident than its current pan-Canadian counterpart. For Québec has an assurance of identity, along with a relative lack of aggressiveness, which are the result of that one major factor of national durability lacking in the rest of Canada: a different language and the cultural fabric that goes with it.

Now how does the Parti Québécois see this society begin to find its way as an independent nation? What is the general outline of the political, social and economic structure we hope to bring forth? Serious observers have been calling our program basically social-democratic, rather comparable to the Scandinavian models although certainly not a carbon copy since all people, through their own experiences, have to invent their own "mix."

The way we have been trying to rough it out democratically through half a dozen national party conventions, ours would call for a presidential regime, as much of an equal-opportunity social system as we could afford, and a decent measure, as quickly as possible but as carefully as indicated, of economic "repatriation." This last would begin to happen immediately, and normally without any great perturbation, through the very fact of sovereignty: with the gathering in of all of our public revenues and the full legislative control which any self-respecting national state has to implement over its main financial institutions, banks, insurance companies and the like. In the latter case, this would allow us to break the stranglehold in which the old British-inspired banking system of just a handful of "majors" has always kept the people's money and financial initiative. The dominant position in our repatriated financial circuit would be handed over to Québec's cooperative institutions, which happen to be particularly well developed in that very field, and, being strongly organized on a regional basis, would afford our population a decent chance for better-balanced, responsible, democratic development. And that, by the way, is just one fundamental aspect of the kind of evolution toward a new economic democracy, from the lowest rung in the marketplace up to board-room levels, which all advanced societies that are not already doing so had better start thinking about in the very near future.

As to non-resident enterprise, apart from the universal minimums concerning incorporations and due respect for Québec taxes, language and other classic national requirements, what we have been fashioning over the last few years is an outline of a policy which we think is both logical and promising. It would take the form of an "investment code," giving a clean-cut picture, by sectors, of what parts of our economic life (e.g., culturally oriented activities, basic steel and forest resources) we would insist on keeping under home ownership, what other parts we would like to see under mixed control (a very few selected but strategic cases) and, finally, the multitude of fields (tied to markets, and to technological and/or capital necessities) where foreign interests would be allowed to stay or to enter provided they do not tend to own us along with their businesses.

In brief, Québec's most privileged links, aside from its most essential relationship with the Canadian partner, would be first with the United States—where there is no imaginable reason to frown on such a tardy but natural and healthy development (especially during a Bicentennial year). Then Québec would look to other Francophone or "Latin" countries as cultural respondents, and to France herself— who would certainly not be indifferent to the fact that this new nation would constitute the second most important French-speaking country in the world. In brief, such is the peaceful and, we confidently hope, fruitfully progressive state which may very well appear on the map of North America before the end of the decade.

QUÉBEC, OUI [4]

He was an unlikely-looking revolutionary. A small, baldish man with tiers of sharply etched bags drooping beneath

[4] Article by Raymond Carroll, a general editor of *Newsweek*, and Jon Lowell, free lance writer in Montreal. *Newsweek*. 88:41-2. N. 29, '76. Copyright 1976 by Newsweek, Inc. All rights reserved. Reprinted by permission.

worried eyes, René Lévesque impassively chain-smoked cigarettes as his excited followers crowded into Montreal's Paul Sauvé arena last week [in November 1976] to await the returns from Quebec's crucial election. As the candidates of Lévesque's separatist Parti Québécois (PQ) racked up victory after victory in races for the provincial Parliament, the crowd roared its approval; many, with tears streaming down their faces, burst into the party song "Tomorrow Belongs to Us." Not until the PQ gained a solid majority of seats did Lévesque decide to speak. Clutching the microphones before him, the 54-year-old former journalist declared: "Now we hope to build this country of Quebec." But Lévesque added, almost anxiously, that the PQ was in no hurry to reach its most cherished goal: a free and independent Quebec.

In fact, the PQ's triumph in no way heralded Quebec's separation from Canada in the near future. Lévesque admitted that it would take quite some time to win a majority of Quebec's people to his cause and then overcome the formidable political obstacles on the road to independence. Nor was it even certain that *la belle province,* the largest in Canada, could even stand on its own as an independent state. Nevertheless, in casting out a Liberal Party government that had governed Quebec since 1970, Lévesque dealt a serious blow to the national government of Liberal Prime Minister Pierre Elliott Trudeau—and quite possibly created a turning point in the history of Canada.

The magnitude of the PQ's victory surprised even Lévesque's most ardent supporters. Three years ago, the party captured 30 per cent of the vote and won only six seats in the provincial Parliament. This time around, the PQ romped off with 41 per cent of the vote and 69 of the 110 seats. The Liberals took only 33 per cent of the votes and saw their 102 seats melt to a humiliating 28. A third party, the right-wing Union Nationale, won 19 per cent of the votes and eleven seats. Despite the turnabout, few Canadians —not even Lévesque himself—viewed the result as a mandate for independence. Polls showed only 18 per cent of Quebec's population favoring independence. During the campaign, the left-of-center PQ played down its separatist goals and concentrated on provincial issues, attacking Liberal Premier Robert Bourassa's government for Quebec's 10.1 per cent unemployment rate and alleged corruption in government.

Objectives

In the aftermath of his victory. Lévesque trod softly, stating that his immediate goals were financial recovery and an honest government within the "present structure." But the small-town lawyer's son from the isloated Gaspé peninsula made it clear that independence remained his long-term objective. Lévesque was expected to ask Quebec's new Parliament for the authority to negotiate with the federal government in Ottawa for a gradual transfer of sovereignty. The PQ leader then intends to keep prodding the federal government, and—possibly within two years—hold a referendum in Quebec to test sentiment for independence. If the vote comes up *non*, Lévesque has indicated, he will wait for better conditions and then call for another referendum.

The possibility that Quebec might go its own way had already persuaded a few English-speaking residents to leave the province. In Ottawa, Prime Minister Trudeau—whose government was in deep trouble after a series of Cabinet resignations, unpopular wage-price controls and an English-speaking backlash against the expanded use of the French language in government—viewed the election results with dismay. A staunch defender of federalism against the separatism of his native Quebec, he had failed all too evidently to rally his own people against the Quebec Party. Still, Trudeau promised to fight. "We have only one mandate," he said of his Liberal government. "It is to govern the whole country, including Quebec. . . . We do not intend to negotiate any form of separatism with any province."

Culture

Officials in Ottawa also doubted that Quebec would be viable as an independent state. True, the province has its own distinctive culture and life-style. It has vast reserves of raw materials and electric power, a healthy furniture industry and high-technology aerospace and electronics industries. It is happily situated, with outlets to the Atlantic ocean via the St. Lawrence River and the Hudson Strait, as well as a commercially valuable border with the U.S.

Canada experts, however, assume that English Canadian capital would desert an independent Quebec and that the all-important U.S. money market would go into a holding pattern until the new country demonstrated its stability. Moreover, since Quebec already has a 1976 budgetary deficit of $1 billion, and since it now gets more back in federal money than it pays Ottawa in taxes, it would have to raise its own taxes or cut services—neither of which would have much appeal for the Québécois. "The bourgeois inclination among French Canadians is stronger than their nationalism," says Dr. Frank Kunz of McGill University. "They would not give up their life-style for a flag."

Pipe Dreams

Even some of the most dedicated backers of the PQ nevertheless feel that complete independence, including a separate army, monetary system and foreign policy, is a pipe dream. Some PQ officials talk of a "middle road" for Quebec that would be neither the status quo nor total independence. "We will end up sharing the same money, the same diplomacy and the same army," remarked one separatist. "I don't see Canada blowing up, I see it becoming more regionalized."

Even if René Lévesque and the PQ come to accept a large degree of "regionalization" rather than outright independence, the shift would not make the federalists in Ottawa much happier. Some of the western provinces, convinced that they are being drained of their wealth by the federal government, might be willing to follow Quebec's lead if the goal were regionalization—more political and economic freedom within the federal framework. If such a trend were to take hold, said the *Toronto Star,* "the western provinces will be tempted by the United States, the Maritime states [Nova Scotia, New Brunswick, and Prince Edward Island] will be cast adrift, Ontario will lose its markets in the rest of Canada and be forced into greater dependence on the U.S." What would emerge from all this ferment was difficult to foresee, but the next decade would almost certainly be a crucial one for the cause of Quebec separatism, regionalism in general, and the future of the Canadian federation.

IV. CANADA'S ECONOMY

EDITOR'S INTRODUCTION

Two areas of economic concern to Canada have grown in importance since the early 1970s. One is the high level of U.S. involvement in Canada's economy; the other is the realization that the Canadian supply of natural resources is not inexhaustible. Canada's reaction to these concerns has been the formulation of a federal policy of economic nationalism—the belief that the needs of Canada must be met before those of any other country, especially the United States.

The Canadian economic scene of the 1970s is put into perspective in this section's first article, which is by Herbert E. Meyer, an associate editor for *Fortune* magazine. The next article concerns the growing reluctance of Canadians to sell more land to foreigners, while the following one deals with the increasing hostility felt in a county in northern Washington toward the influx of Canadians who are purchasing land in the area.

Canada's relationship to the United States vis-à-vis the energy situation is covered in the next two articles. The first of these is an interview with Canadian Minister of Finance Donald S. Macdonald, who at the time was minister of energy, mines and resources; in the interview Macdonald formalizes Canada's nationalist policy toward its energy-related resources. The second, which is from the *Wall Street Journal*, demonstrates that the potential for American-Canadian cooperation on a large scale does still exist.

The manner in which Prime Minister Pierre Elliott Trudeau has attempted to manage Canada's problems of inflation are noted in this section's final piece, taken from a syndicated column by Joseph Kraft.

NATIONALISM AND CANADA'S ECONOMY [1]

. . . [Since 1972], the Canadian government has been trying to loosen Canada's economic ties to the U.S. The effort has met with only modest success; some of the ties between the two countries seem tighter today than they were in 1972. But it is increasingly clear that attempts to loosen the U.S. connection have vastly expanded the role of government in the Canadian economy. In fact, Canadian businessmen are now worried that the price of economic nationalism may be their own freedom of operation.

The concentration of economic control and policy in the hands of a highly centralized government has come at a time when the economy is dangerously weak. Rising wage rates, high inflation, and low productivity gains are all eating away at Canada's export position, especially in the U.S. market. That's bad news indeed for a country whose economic health rests so completely upon its ability to sell products abroad.

Economic trouble is especially dangerous for Canada because any sustained decline in the general standard of living must inevitably aggravate the internal political struggles—among the ten provinces, and between the provinces and Ottawa—that has always kept this vast, resource-wealthy land from realizing its extraordinary potential. The provinces are so different, so independent, so much at odds with each other and with Ottawa, that it is hardly an exaggeration to describe Canada not as a country, but rather as an idea for a country that has not yet come into being.

The Middle of the Road Is Empty

The divisions among the provinces are of several kinds —cultural and economic as well as political. . . . A lot of people in Quebec, and elsewhere in Canada, want to see

[1] From "Canada's Nationalism Exacts a High Price," by Herbert E. Meyer, an associate editor of *Fortune*; research associate: Susie Gharib Nazem. *Fortune.* 94: 179-83+. Ag. '76. Reprinted from the August 1976 issue of *Fortune* by special permission: © 1976 Time Inc.

this troubled, sometimes violent province leave the confederation. Out in the western provinces, dislike for Quebec is exceeded only by the distrust and even loathing felt for Ontario, the richest and most powerful province. With 42 percent of Canada's manufacturing and 28 percent of its farm income, Ontario is regarded elsewhere in the country with the mixture of jealousy and contempt some Americans have for New York, only more so.

Politically, the middle of the road is a fairly empty place in Canada's provinces. Voters in British Columbia elected a socialist government in 1972 (and voted it out in 1975), and a socialist government in Saskatchewan is taking over the province's potash mines. But Alberta, in the Rocky Mountain region, has vast oil reserves, and a government that is as capitalistic and growth-oriented as they come. To a degree that often surprises Americans who mistakenly equate Canadian provinces with U.S. states, the provinces have the political power to set their own courses. They often do it with little regard for each other, and less for Ottawa. Think of Canada as a collection of notes; do not think of it as music.

As so often happens when a country is divided internally, an overpowering urge develops to unite against a common enemy or what is perceived as one. For Canadians, the large, powerful, and dynamic U.S. has always been a most appealing villain. It is close enough to put the smaller country in a permanent shadow, big enough to hit at will, and too big to really feel the blows or become angry enough to hit back.

Canadians have been tweaking the eagle's tail feathers for a century, but it was not until 1972 that the government made nationalism an official policy. Since this policy is utterly devoted to permanently changing the U.S.-Canadian relationship, it is especially important to understand the Canadian perception of this relationship as it now stands. Prime Minister Pierre Trudeau is fond of describing Canada as a mouse in bed with an elephant, and the analogy is not without merit. U.S. companies control 36 percent of Canada's paper and pulp industry, 43 percent of its mining and smelting industry, 45 percent of its manufacturing industry, and 58 percent of its oil and natural-gas industry. Of the 100 largest companies in Canada, forty are American-owned.

It is a cliché in Canada that extensive U.S. investment, which totals about $30 billion, has turned the country into a branch-plant economy. Sixty-six percent of Canada's $32 billion worth of exports in 1975 went to the U.S. And of the $34.6 billion of goods and services that Canada imported . . . [in 1975], 68 percent came from the U.S. This makes Canada by far the United States' best trading partner. So tight is this partnership that the two economies have historically performed in tandem, the smaller one trailing the larger by several months. Canadian economists say they look at the U.S. to see where they are going, and U.S. economists can look north to see where they've just been.

America's cultural influence in Canada is as pervasive as its economic influence. An overwhelming majority of books and magazines sold at Canadian newsstands are of U.S. origin. Since 90 percent of all Canadians live within 200 miles of the U.S. border, American television shows are readily available and extremely popular. American films and hit records fairly dominate the Canadian market, and virtually every brand-name American product is available to Canadian shoppers.

The Talent Moved South

Canadian nationalists argue that America's overwhelming influence and wealth often work to Canada's disadvantage. They point out, accurately, that U.S. companies with plants in Canada have a tendency to lay off workers at those plants before cutting back production at plants in the States. And they complain that the higher salaries and vastly greater opportunities for advancement available in the U.S., especially in the worlds of business and art, have drained Canada of some top-quality talent that might otherwise have stayed at home and contributed to Canada's development and glory.

John Kenneth Jamieson, the former chairman of Exxon, was born and raised in Medicine Hat. [Industrialist] Cyrus Eaton was a Canadian, too. So were James L. Kraft, who came to Chicago in 1903 and founded a cheese company, Alfred C. Fuller, who arrived the same year and got into brushes, and Elizabeth Arden, who was born in Ontario. The list of Canadian-Americans includes John Kenneth Galbraith, the economist; S. I. Hayakawa, formerly president of San Francisco State College and now a . . . [member of] the U.S. Senate, and novelist Saul Bellow. Raymond Massey, the actor, comes from the Toronto family that founded Massey-Ferguson, the farm-machinery company. Mary Pickford was born in Canada, and so was Jay Silverheels, better known to a generation of Americans as the Lone Ranger's Tonto.

The tendency of U.S. companies to shut down their Canadian plants first is irritating and obviously unpleasant for Canadian workers, but thoughtful Canadians understand that if it had not been for U.S. investment, those jobs would probably not have been there in the first place. And they readily admit that Messrs. Kraft and Fuller could not have built their empires in a market as small as Canada's; that nothing could have kept an actor destined to portray *Abe Lincoln in Illinois* away from Broadway and Hollywood. In fact, all but the most fanatical Canadian nationalists concede that their country's close relationship with the U.S. has, on balance, been a very profitable one for Canada. They know full well that only by riding the back of the powerful U.S. economy has their country of just 22 million people—roughly the population of California—been able to achieve a standard of living that equals the U.S. standard.

The problem with the U.S.-Canadian relationship is not so much what it is today, Canadians emphasize, but rather with what it might become. They argue that no intelligent mouse, however warm and comfortable, can be blind to the awful possibility of being injured or even crushed should the elephant beside it get angry, or simply forget the mouse is there and roll over on it. Fair enough. But how best can the mouse assure its safety?

Gravity at Edge of the Bed

In the fall of 1972, Mitchell Sharp, then Canada's secretary of state for external affairs, outlined three options for Canada. The first was to maintain the country's existing relationship with the U.S. and, so to speak, hope for the best. The second was to move deliberately toward even closer integration with the U.S., which would increase the risk but also increase the benefits. And the third option—the one Sharp told Canadians their government was adopting as the cornerstone of its policy—was "to pursue a comprehensive long-term strategy to develop and strengthen the Canadian economy and other aspects of its natural life and in the process to reduce the present Canadian vulnerability." In language less diplomatic, Canada was going to move its pillow further toward the edge of the bed.

Now, one need not actually have had the experience of sleeping with an elephant to recognize that any attempt to move toward the bed's edge would be an uphill struggle. Gravity pulls you back toward the center. Likewise for any Canadian effort to put some distance between Canada and the U.S., for the American economy and culture have an almost gravitational attraction to many Canadians and Canadian organizations.

Moreover, nationalism was by no means the only force at work in Canada. The provinces were pulling in assorted directions, and the country's business community actively opposed the third option. Most businessmen favored letting market forces determine the U.S.-Canadian relationship, and those forces were likely to make the links even tighter. In any case, Canadian businessmen had neither the capital nor the inclination to buy out U.S.-owned companies; only the government could afford to do it. But the federal government would need much more power than it had to make the third-option policy work—enough power to overcome any opposition and attain sufficient thrust to blast Canada beyond the gravitational reach of the U.S.

"The System Is Out of Joint"

The man at the vortex of all the forces in Canada—rather like the sun around which all the planets in a galaxy revolve—is Pierre Elliott Trudeau, the controversial, contradictory, undeniably charismatic prime minister whose policies and personality have dominated Canadian political life since 1968. Today, because of Canada's economic troubles, even more attention than usual is focused on the prime minister. After winning the 1974 elections largely on his opposition to the idea of controls on wages and profits, he stunned the country last October 13 [1975] by imposing them.

When the controls program was announced, most Canadians assumed that Trudeau's only purpose was to provide a shock that would somehow jolt the economy off its downward course. He put a 12 percent ceiling on wage increases, and companies were ordered to reduce their profit margins to a ceiling equal to 95 percent of those margins during the last five years. This percentage has since been lowered further, to 85 percent.

It was not until the closing days of 1975 that Canadians learned how their prime minister viewed the controls program—not as a temporary evil, but rather as a prelude to permanent changes in the role of government in Canada. The occasion was a year-end television interview. A comment by Trudeau that the need for controls proved "the system is out of joint" prompted an interviewer to ask whether the prime minister thought "bigness" was the source of Canada's economic problems.

Trudeau agreed that it was, and then went on to explain precisely what he had in mind to do about it. "We can't destroy the big unions and we can't destroy the multinationals," he said. "We can control them—but who can control them? The government. This means that government is going to take a larger role in running institutions . . . even after the controls are ended. . . . It means there's going to be not less authority in our lives but perhaps more."

In . . . [an] interview with *Fortune* [magazine], Trudeau talked about his philosophy and about his plans to expand the role of government in the Canadian economy. . . . Trudeau [is] a slightly built, athletic man who looks much younger than his age (fifty-six). . . . A former law professor and the son of a millionaire businessman—his father, a lawyer, owned an auto-service business, said to be worth $1.4 million, that he sold to Imperial Oil in 1931—Trudeau is obviously comfortable in the job he has held for eight tumultuous years. He leaves no doubt that he intends to pursue his policies despite opposition from businessmen—especially bankers.

The Sound of Galbraith

"When they put me in the bag as a socialist, I begin to wonder if they're kidding or if their vision of socialism isn't so wide that they'd accept only an Adam Smith liberal," the prime minister said heatedly. "Do they honestly think our economy can work in an absolutely free market? It's obvious that we don't have a pure free market in Canada and probably never did."

Although Trudeau denies he has been much influenced by the works of John Kenneth Galbraith, his analysis of how large corporations and big unions connive to circumvent market forces matches the Galbraith analysis almost to the word. "If the free-market system worked well," argues Trudeau, "in areas of overproduction or economic slowdown, companies would be cutting prices and cutting their salaries—which they're not. The corporations themselves are not obeying the rules of the market. The consumer is not, in a period of slowdown, buying cheaper goods. He's buying at the same price. And there are fewer layoffs, and certainly you don't see wages going down any more in a period of recession. Presumably there's a sweetheart deal between some unions and some corporations to pass the costs on to the consumers and keep the prices up."

In Trudeau's view, businessmen object to government intervention only when the government's actions are not the ones that businessmen want. "In the same week that the bankers were complaining that I was interfering in the market system, there was a group of bankers enjoining us to change the Bank Act to give them much greater protection [from competition]. . . . So how can you expect me to take them seriously when they say the government shouldn't be regulating the economy?"

Trudeau believes that it is the responsibility of government to step in where free enterprise fails—in the area of matching people with jobs. "We've got high inflation and high unemployment in our industrialized societies. In Canada's case we've got unemployment at 6.9 percent now and we've got inflation down to 8.9 percent. Both we consider too high. How do you put the unemployed to work? Is the market putting these unemployed together with the work that needs to be done?

"And what do the bankers say about that? I'll tell you what they say. They say the government should step back. It's too much meddling that is causing these problems. My hands fall at that point. If they think the coexistence of high inflation and high unemployment is Pierre Trudeau's fault, well, it's happening in other countries, some of which are socialist, some of which are Tory, some of which are republican, some of which are liberal. It's a problem not solved by ideological accusations." But the prime minister lets loose one scathing accusation of his own: "The worst bitchers of all are the bankers. They've never had it so good as under my government. I'm ashamed they've been making profits way ahead of the secondary manufacturing and service sector, the industrial sector, and the natural-resource sector."

Trudeau's reasoning has led him to the belief that "structural changes" need to be made in Canada's economic system. "The public interest requires government to play a coordinating role in economic planning," he says. "The changes we will make are designed to enable government to play this role. . . ."

Ottawa Constructs a Forum

A few details about those impending changes have been revealed by other government officials. Donald S. Macdonald, Trudeau's powerful and ebullient finance minister, says Ottawa plans to increase its powers to regulate a wide range of business activities—especially the activities of banks, including foreign banks operating in Canada. In addition, says Macdonald, the federal government will vote itself increased powers to "coordinate" access by private corporations and provincial governments to the capital markets.

One of Macdonald's colleagues in the Cabinet, Donald Jamieson, [former] minister of industry, trade, and commerce [who in September 1976 was named secretary of state for external affairs], says that the planned structural changes will give Ottawa a big role in "priority setting" for the entire process of economic development. Jamieson is certainly not about to leave something as important as economic development to Canada's business community. The minister . . . told a group of Dallas executives that most Canadian companies "are small and have limited management talent and financial influence, which calls for substantial government involvement in their affairs."

The groundwork for all these structural changes is being done by a committee of ten deputy ministers. One member of this powerful group, called the DM-10 committee, is Thomas Eberlee, deputy minister of labor. Eberlee says the new structure will essentially be a "tripartite" forum comprised of government, organized labor, and business. "We will soon see new relationships emerging among these groups," Eberlee predicts. Among Canadian bureaucrats, the word "tripartite" is heard almost as often as "third option" these days.

Here Comes Canada Inc.

While the organizational details of tripartitism still remain to be completed and announced—at first blush, the idea sounds like a cross between [such similar plans as] West Germany's *Mitbestimmung* and the Soviet Union's GOSPLAN—it is easy to see how such a system would vastly expand the federal government's powers to plan and coordinate Canada's economic growth. Neither private companies nor provincial governments would be able to run their affairs without Ottawa's approval. By controlling access to the capital markets, for example, the federal government could reward some companies, punish others, and force construction of new plants wherever the authorities want them built. And so long as the controls program remains in effect (it expires December 31, 1978, and Trudeau says that only a "miracle" would induce him to end it sooner) the government can force adjustments in wages and profits whenever it likes.

Tripartitism is the culmination of Trudeau's drive to increase the power of the federal government. That dovetails neatly with his effort to loosen ties to the U.S., because the third option's objectives cannot be accomplished until Ottawa gets the authority to guide and direct the country's economy. Tripartitism is a way to knit a weak, loosely connected group of provinces and private enterprises into a coherent, rational, manageable organization—a sort of Canada Inc., with the prime minister as chairman of the board.

The third option had been opposed from the start by some provincial governments. Quebec, for example, wants tighter economic links to the U.S. in hopes of attracting investment that would create jobs. "We are among the poorest provinces in Canada," explains Robert Bourassa, Quebec's intense, French-speaking [former] premier. "We want foreign investment here. We need the jobs such investments will bring." Bourassa regularly visits the U.S. "You are welcome here," he says, over and over again. "Please, come and build plants in Quebec."

Alberta, which produces 85 percent of Canada's oil, also wants closer ties with the U.S. The province currently produces 1.2 million barrels a day, and its ultimately recoverable reserves have been estimated at 262 billion barrels (including vast quantities in expensive-to-process tar sands). That's more than the proven reserves of Saudi Arabia, and the province seeks American investment so that it can get its oil out of the ground while prices are high. In the booming oil towns of Calgary and Edmonton, Pierre Trudeau's third option is viewed as a dirty trick to keep Albertans from getting rich.

The opposition of provincial governments to the third option has been a serious problem for Trudeau, because the provinces have been able to set their own courses independently of Ottawa's direction. The source of their power is a document written in another country, in another century. The British North America Act of 1867 established the federal-provincial relationship in Canada. In composing the document, the British Parliament gave most powers to the provincial governments, leaving Ottawa in a relatively weak position.

The Provinces Are Tightfisted

The 1867 act, which stands today as Canada's constitution, contained a time bomb that exploded at precisely that moment when Trudeau launched his third option. All mineral resources are owned by the provincial governments. That ownership was not a great source of power before 1972. But when the age of shortages arrived, and with it skyrocketing prices for virtually anything that came from the ground, some of Canada's provinces found themselves on the threshold of extraordinary wealth. They were not inclined to be generous about sharing the wealth with Ottawa or the other provinces.

In setting out to take over the eleven potash mines that

are operating within its borders, the government of Saskatchewan, a midwest farming province, aims to get control over deposits representing 40 percent of the world's potash reserves. Last year the mines, mostly American-owned, poured $100 million of royalties and taxes into Saskatchewan's coffers. But the Trudeau government opposed the takeover, though the result would be a broken link with the U.S. Ottawa argued that the profits should go to the federal government to redistribute as it saw fit. Saskatchewan, in effect, told Ottawa to buzz off, and is going ahead with the takeover.

A similar battle for mineral-resource wealth developed between the Trudeau government and the Pacific northwest province of British Columbia. As prices zoomed for British Columbia's copper and zinc, the provincial government in Victoria boosted mining taxes and royalties to the point where Ottawa, once again, felt it was being cut out of the money. Trudeau responded by raising the federal mining tax rates and by declaring that provincial taxes and royalties would no longer be deductible. As a result of this particular struggle for revenue, the effective tax rate for some mining companies in British Columbia exceeded 100 percent. In 1975, Gibraltar Mines Ltd., a Vancouver-based affiliate of Noranda Mines, earned $1,633,000; its taxes that year totaled $2,009,000.

Ottawa's most potent weapon in its struggle with the provinces for control over mineral resources is the Canada Development Corporation. This government company was established in 1971 to invest in Canadian-controlled corporations and give them a chance to grow. But C.D.C.'s mission soon widened. In July, 1973, it made a tender offer for 30 percent of the shares of Texasgulf Inc., the giant U.S. mining company with extensive Caanadian properties. The buy-back stunned the U.S. and Canadian business communities, and cost Canadian taxpayers $271 million. It effectively transferred control of the American company to the Canadian government.

Last year came the formation of Petro-Canada, a government-owned oil company whose purpose, the prime minister said, was to provide Ottawa with a "window" into the country's foreign-controlled energy industry. But Petro-Can soon abandoned that modest pretense and began to expand rapidly into a major oil company with multinational connections. Its chairman, Maurice F. Strong, a highly successful oilman, has already held preliminary discussions on deals with Venezuela and North Vietnam. "We now have an international mandate," Strong insists.

Petro-Can started off with $500 million in equity and the right to borrow $1 billion more over the next five years with government backing. Regulations announced in May by the Ministry of Energy, Mines, and Resources give the company some roaring advantages over private companies. For example, it now has the right to explore any open federal acreage that isn't developed by private companies during the next seven years.

Another new rule requires that all new exploration ventures on federal acreage be at least 25 percent Canadian-owned. Since Petro-Can is the only big Canadian-owned oil company in the country, the rule will force private companies to take on the government as a partner. And in a further extension of its power, Petro-Can announced plans in June to buy the Canadian subsidiary of Atlantic Richfield for $335 million.

It's Not the Principle

Like the provincial governments, the Canadian business community has consistently opposed Trudeau's third-option policy. Most Canadian businessmen have been more concerned with the health of their country's economy than with the nationality of its owners. And at just about the same time that Trudeau launched the third option, the Canadian economy was beginning to weaken. As Paul H. Leman, the president of Alcan Aluminum, puts it: "We caught a bad case of the English sickness." Wage rates, for example, went up so high, so fast, that by 1975, Northern Telecom Ltd., a subsidiary of Bell Canada, was paying $1.85 per hour more to its Canadian workers than to its U.S. employees. In the paper and pulp industry, wages in Canada rose to nearly $1 per hour more than in the U.S.

Canadian businessmen are reacting by doing exactly the reverse of what the Trudeau government wants them to do. They are allowing market forces rather than political considerations to guide them, and those forces lead them to tighten the U.S.-Canadian connection Ottawa is so anxious to break. "We've done a magnificent job of making ourselves uncompetitive internationally" is the very bitter conclusion of Robert C. Scrivener, chairman of Northern Telecom. "Canadians are now being paid more to work less efficiently than their counterparts in the U.S. Our competitive position has eroded to the point where we're seeing the ultimate irony: Canadian companies starting up plants in the U.S., so they may compete in the Canadian market."

Last year Dominion Textile Ltd., a Montreal-based company with annual sales of $273 million, bought a U.S. textile company called DHJ Industries Inc. that operates ten plants in the States. Domtex says its operating costs for these plants are 15 to 20 percent lower than for its similar plants in Canada. The company has warned shareholders that "as our plants reach obsolescence they are not being replaced here in Canada."

Some Noranda Mines affiliates have slashed their budgets for mineral exploration in Canada by as much as 50 percent, and put the money into U.S. exploration projects. Dominion Bridge Co., a Montreal structural-steel manufacturer, is also weakening its ties to Canada—its principal officers are now based in New Hampshire, and the company is expanding in the U.S. "Canada was pricing itself out of the world markets and we weren't prepared to sit there and see this happen," explains Kenneth S. Barclay, the company's president.

FIRA Shows Its Colors

Today, in a reversal that could mean big trouble for Canada's future development, the flow of investment capital from Canada to the U.S. exceeds the northward flow. This outflow of badly needed capital is likely to increase still further as a result of some recent decisions by the Foreign Investment Review Agency [FIRA], which was established by Trudeau back in 1974 and which is now beginning to show its colors.

The enabling legislation requires foreign-owned companies to obtain FIRA's approval before starting a new company in Canada, buying a Canadian company, or expanding into a new line of business. Only if FIRA deems the project to be "of significant benefit to Canada" is the application approved. But now FIRA is using this vague, very broad authority to force U.S. companies into selling their Canadian subsidiaries back to Canadians.

When Gulf & Western Industries acquired the U.S. publishing firm of Simon & Schuster in June, 1975, FIRA ruled that the publishing firm's Canadian subsidiary Simon & Schuster of Canada Ltd., could not be transferred to the new owners. Gulf & Western had to sell off the subsidiary to a Canadian buyer.

FIRA's actions, combined with Ottawa's other policies and the Saskatchewan potash takeover, have led American businessmen with interests in Canada to start asking, "What's the political risk factor up there?" Some have already decided that it's too high. Robert E. Naegele, president of Dow Chemical of Canada, says his company is seriously thinking of abandoning plans to build a petrochemical plant in Alberta.

Labor's Route to Power

Trudeau's term of office ends in 1978, and he must call an election sometime before then. But even if he were thrown out of office, his successor would find it difficult to reverse the present policies. Both government control of the economy and nationalism remain extremely popular with Canadian voters. A public-opinion survey published in May showed that a majority considers U.S. economic and cultural influence to be a "major source of concern." The new leader of the opposition Conservative party, thirty-seven-year-old Joe Clark, concedes that even if he came to power, "we'd be more inclined to slow things down, rather than reverse them."

As Trudeau pushes ahead with his plans to reshape the Canadian economy, he is welcoming a new, potentially very powerful ally: Canada's labor movement. Its guiding organization is the Canadian Labor Congress [C.L.C.], a fast-growing coalition of militant unions that now represents 36 percent of the country's work force.

Previously no friend of Trudeau, the C.L.C. believes that the policy of tripartism will give labor a much larger role than it now has in planning and managing the country's economy. Ronald Lang, forty-three, C.L.C.'s director of legislation, says the organization views tripartism as its route to power in "all economic affairs" of Canada. "Quite frankly," says Lang, who quit high school at sixteen, started again at thirty-one, and kept on going until he earned a Ph.D. from the London School of Economics, "what we're doing now is organizing ourselves so that when tripartism comes, labor has got the strongest voice at the table."

Events are moving swiftly now, and deep and lasting change in Canada is inevitable as Trudeau pursues his policies. In June, he held the first of a series of meetings with C.L.C. leaders to discuss tripartism. In July, he announced the establishment of a "contractual link" between Canada and the Common Market that he says will pave the way for Canadian businesses to get additional non-American trading partners. The prime minister has been so deeply immersed in projects to push Canada away from the U.S. and to centralize economic power, in fact, that he seems to

give scant thought these days to what Canada will be like
if his efforts prove successful.

FOREIGN LAND OWNERSHIP IN CANADA [2]

We must have priorities in our national worrying and
therefore the bigger controversies have always had more to
do with boardrooms, banks and bilingualism than with cot-
tages, canoes and campfires. In the light of this, it hardly
seemed important a few years ago [during the early 1970s]
that a bunch of loose-spending Bostonians and New Yorkers
were goosing the price of farmland in the Annapolis Valley.
Or that a Dallas fashion king had just bought himself a
chunk of a perfectly darling little island off British Columbia. Or even that a Madison Avenue land hustler was ped-
dling thousands of acres of prime Laurentian playground—
for roughly *eight times* what he'd paid for it—to people
from Oklahoma, Idaho, Wisconsin and Louisiana.

This sort of thing, among Debates of National Importance, was still very small potatoes only three or four years
ago. And why not? No one was doing anything illegal.
Americans have a perfect right to buy land in Canada. Canadians have a perfect right to sell land to whomever they
choose; and, indeed, to hear some politicians and many real
estate wheelers talk, no right is more sacred. And anyway,
beside the economic nationalists' latest figures on the frightening speed with which the Americans had gobbled up
whole Canadian industries, the discovery that Americans
had also gobbled up the whole shore of good old Lake Ona-
wongdangdawa was puny news.

Now, however, foreign ownership of Canadian land is
blossoming as a major and endless issue right across the
country. There's scarcely a province that's not taking a hard
look at the law to see how to control the flow of Canadian
land into foreign hands. Prince Edward Island and Saskatchewan both have laws to limit foreigners' investment

[2] From "Land Grab," by Harry Bruce, a Halifax author and free lance writer.
Maclean's. 88:25-9. My. '75. Reprinted by permission of the author.

in their land. Ontario has a special tax on land transfers to foreigners. And Nova Scotia, in a swooping and unprecedented act of expropriation, announced . . . [in 1974] that it was taking from an Ohio woman more than 5,400 acres of gorgeous South Shore property.

Within the past half-dozen years, Americans, Europeans, Japanese and, more recently, Arab oil kings and Mafia interests have determined that Canada is one beautiful big place in which to put money into land. Many wealthy Europeans fear what a socialist take-over would do to their property at home. They admire the political stability of Canada. The return on investments in Canadian land is high and, perhaps even more important to, say, a West German doctor, the whole investment is safe.

Such considerations apply particularly to the heavily populated and economically high-flying area of southern Ontario, and perhaps, too, to the foreigners' urge to own thousands of acres of prime agricultural land in the Prairies [Manitoba, Saskatchewan, and Alberta].

But in the Atlantic Provinces [New Brunswick, New-foundland, Nova Scotia, Prince Edward Island] in BC [British Columbia], in Quebec's Laurentian country and resort belt of Ontario, the pressure is on from Americans, who will pay more than any of the locals can ever hope to raise. . . .

American cottage-owners may be ideal guests of Canada, generous summertime members of a Canadian community, blameless neighbors and superb groundskeepers. But sometimes the land they buy at what the locals regard as outrageously inflated prices is land these same locals have coveted, land these same locals may even have used for generations into the past.

There are other problems. In some parts of the country, an American's innocent act of paying a fat price for a farm not only takes one more farm out of production but also encourages assessment officials to raise the taxes on neighboring properties. Some of the neighbors may be having a tough enough time keeping their own farms in production anyway and, when the next rich American drops by with a stupendous offer, one of them may accept it. And there goes another farm out of production.

The farmer insists he has a right to sell to the highest bidder. And maybe he has. Moreover, some foreigners . . . insist that, under the Canadian Citizenship Act, they have the same rights as Canadians to buy and sell Canadian land. They have taken the case to the Supreme Court of Canada.

Some real estate experts wonder what the fuss is all about. They argue that if Canada must sell anything to foreigners, why not sell the one thing no one can actually take out of the country. The land will still be here, no matter who owns it.

They miss the emotional point.

Even the most stridently continentalist businessman, when he considers the strip of lakefront forest that's most dear to him, becomes a nationalist. We cannot make the land again. It is not potatoes, sugar, rolls of newsprint, or barrels of oil. It is where we have walked, and where we stand and, like a stubborn farmer whom the Depression has laid low, we have to ask, "If I can no longer call even that my own, what have I got?" This is why the issue has begun to bubble across the country, and why you're likely to see new laws, in assorted provinces, in the months to come. [Since 1975, legislation has been enacted placing restrictions on foreign ownership of land.—Ed.]

THE CANADIANS ARE COMING [3]

"Quite a reversal, isn't it?" sniffed one British Columbian Government official. . . . "For years Americans have been buying big chunks of Canada. Now we buy a little land down in the States and everybody squawks."

They're squawking the loudest in Whatcom County, Washington, just 40 miles from Vancouver. This border

[3] From "The Canadians Are Coming!" by Mary Alice Kellogg, an associate editor in *Newsweek*'s San Francisco bureau. *Nation*. 220:722-4. Je. 14, '75. Copyright 1975 in the U.S.A. by the Nation Associates, Inc. Reprinted with permission.

county of rural farmland, wooded slopes and hundreds of crystal lakes is in the middle of a Canadian-fed recreational land boom that has set local developer pockets jingling and many local residents howling against the invasion. Where once pastoral scenes slumbered for the delight of Whatcom residents on an outing, today hastily constructed recreational subdivisions bulge rudely from the landscape. Cars jam the inadequate highways on weekends, grassy hills have been replaced by golf courses and recreational complexes. "Until five years ago our valley was a decent place to live," laments Mrs. Neila Stewart, a Whatcom resident, "but now I see a lot of confusion, overcrowding and angry people."

Part of the anger stems from Whatcom's own failures. Until . . . [1975], the postcard county was 95 percent unzoned, ripe for helter-skelter development. It was referred to as "wide-open Whatcom." When [former] county planner Harry Fulton, himself a native Canadian and naturalized American, introduced a comprehensive zoning plan . . . [in 1909] his proposals were booed by the residents. After all, why should they have zoning? For more than thirty years, Whatcom's largest town, Bellingham, had been a sleepy place surrounded by tiny farm communities. During the 1950s, Bellingham grew by only 1 per cent. But in the 1960s, that began to change. The town gained 6,000 new residents and watched 9,000 newly arrived suburbanites settle just outside its city limits. Bellingham found it had a population of 40,000, and in six years the countywide population rose by 15,000, to 90,000.

Bellingham did not realize what was happening to it until . . . [1970], when the scars of uncontrolled development began to show. At that time, when Seattle, 130 miles to the south had its big recession, "a lot of cheap builders came up here—and you can see what they've done," says Harry Fulton. Bellingham's graceful Victorian homes with their view of Puget Sound had for new neighbors bland houses which were symbols of a growth people were only beginning to understand.

Builders who had been pushing recreational properties

to the residents of Seattle began to concentrate on Vancouver's population of nearly a million. Hemmed in by rugged mountains on one side and the sea on the other, Vancouverities were running out of land for their holiday retreats. A land freeze instituted by British Columbia in 1972 reduced the amount of available recreational and residential land and pushed Canadian property values to the groaning point. Whatcom County became a bargain.

Consequences of the Canadian Influx

. . . [In 1975] in Whatcom there are seven major recreational developments, none of which is five years old. Of the 12,000 lots, the vast majority are owned by Canadians. Sudden Valley, a development 10 miles from Bellingham on Lake Whatcom, is 85 per cent Canadian-owned, with lots selling from $7,000 to $32,000. Paradise Lakes Country Club, in Neila Stewart's Columbia Valley, is 88 per cent Canadian-owned. The Whatcom treasurer says that nearly one-third of all real estate sales for the first eight months of 1974—$27 million worth—were to Canadian purchasers. Seventy-five per cent of lots sold have gone to people from north of the border, and local real estate value has jumped 15 per cent in a year, making county assessor Lewis Turner's job a giant headache. "Raw land that sold for $200 to $300 an acre five or six years ago will easily get $1,000 an acre today."

That's still a bargain. Prices for homes and land in Whatcom are at least 30 per cent (and in most cases, 50 per cent) below those of British Columbia. Homes that cost $65,000 in the province go for about $40,000 in Whatcom. Twenty per cent of the property owners in the county are Canadian, and they pay 5 per cent of the total real estate tax. The dollar value of real estate transactions has more than doubled since 1970, to more than $121 million . . . [in 1974].

All these percentages and profits have made a very considerable dent in Whatcom County. "The attitude of the public has changed drastically . . . ," says planner Fulton. His comprehensive zoning plan, which had been lying in the basement of county offices since 1969, was enthusiastically dusted off in 1972. Last fall [1974], two new members of the Board of Commissioners won their seats on a campaign advocating zoning and attacking the subdivision of agricultural land. Last year [1974], a land-use code committee was formed, its members a cross section of the community. The fifty citizens on the committee were to deal with the problems of rampant development.

In practical terms, the Canadian land rush has been a mixed blessing. Downtown Bellingham merchants report that 30 per cent of their business is with Canadians. The American developers of Whatcom land are required by law to hire only U.S. citizens for construction work. Operators of local recreational vehicle franchises report their business is flourishing, thanks to Canadians.

But with this prosperity the Canadians bring their urban ills. Highways leading to the major developments are crammed on weekends; recreational services are overburdened. Ken Hertz, director of the Whatcom park system, thinks "the pressure for county park facilities by Canadians is going to reach the point of political decision: should we keep the Canadians out? The feeling of many people I talk to is one of open animosity. I think some day we'll see the commissioners run on a platform of keeping Canadians out."

In a . . . survey of county park users (in some areas, like snowcapped Mount Baker, 90 per cent are Canadian), Whatcom residents clearly indicated what they thought was wrong. Fifty-two per cent said the "greatest problem" with the park system was its use by noncounty residents, specifically Canadians. To deal with increasing numbers of visitors, the county parks have had to institute a reservation system (county residents get first choice for campsites that previously were abundant and uncluttered) and non-county residents pay a $1 per-car fee.

"I've seen the anti-Canadian feeling grow," says Hertz. "There's not a chance in hell we can stop Canadians from coming over here. The feeling seems to be that if we can't do that, we should limit Canadian land purchasing capabilities." That is not as easy as it would appear: in order to stop Canadians from owning land, the Washington state constitution would have to be changed. One state legislator is currently gathering information on land purchase by "foreigners" to check the feasibility of such a step, but for now the only restrictions are through tough zoning for the developments. There is a feeling in Whatcom that not enough has been done. "I don't think the county is doing a good job in solidly zoning the land," says Hertz. "They could be providing more regulatory methods. It is possible to control this, if people realize we will have a certain amount of this crap until they wake up."

A "Canadian" Land Boom

This is a land boom in which egos have been bruised. "The Canadian used to be the guy in the little beat-up cheap car, kind of a poor country cousin, who would come for a visit," says Harry Fulton. "But now he's the big shot in a big long Cadillac with lots and lots of money to spend." Neila Stewart, who has formed a citizens' group to stop real estate development, tries to couch it in gentler terms: "We're not against Canadians as a people. We're against noise, overcrowding and pollution—which is what these developments bring. This is our home, and what is happening to it is heartbreaking. The commissioners aren't looking at the problem closely enough. We think it's wrong to sell off land to a foreign country."

As can be guessed, the commissioners are caught between the business advantages on the one side and irate citizens on the other. "As we zone, we zone for the benefit and use of the whole county," wearily sighs C. J. ("Corky") Johnson, chairman of the board. "We can't restrict potential customers to Americans only. We'd badly crimp the county economy if we did that." Johnson admits that Whatcom is "a developer's paradise . . . ," and also allows that Canadians seem to be the only ones buying. "They have the money and the Vancouver resident has no place to go," he says. "We're faced with a hell of a mess."

Also faced with a mess are U.S. Immigration officials, who are currently saddled with heavy weekend border traffic and the thankless job of trying to weed out Canadians illegally living in the United States and working in Canada. The waiting list for a visa to work in the United States is currently two and a half years for Canadians. "It's a tragic situation," says Immigration official Harry Klajbor of the Blaine, Washington border station. "Nobody tells them, in many cases, that they have to have a visa to live here and work in Canada. People are buying homes and don't know this." Klajbor's department is currently conducting an educational campaign to let Canadians know the restrictions, but there are still cases of deportation—eight . . . [in 1974].

Weekend lines across the border have grown to ridiculous proportions. What used to be a twenty-minute wait to get across has turned into a 2-mile line of cars. "It might get to the point where it is an impossible situation to control," sighs Klajbor. "Everybody knows what the problems are, but there aren't any answers. Nobody takes an overall look at the situation. How do you cut off foreign ownership? Who will do it? The problem isn't going to get any smaller."

For its part, the government of British Columbia doesn't seem too much concerned. "I don't think the politics of British Columbia has created the situation so much as the geography of British Columbia," says [former] B.C. Land Commission Chairman William Lane. "You have half of our population living in the southwest corner of the province with a density close to that of Belgium and a twenty-year history of land-use controls. Across the border you have more habitable land, with a history of little or no land-use control. Of course there's a certain temptation when you put the two side by side." Lane does not view the situation as serious, saying: "I don't think there's a shortage of recreational property in the province, anyway. The people of Whatcom County should look to their own best interests.

The citizens there have not had strong reason for land-use control, and now there is a conflict. British Columbians aren't in any way offended if they want to zone."

And zone they may. With Canada's fastest-growing province just across the border (British Columbia is responsible for one-fourth of Canada's growth . . .) and their own state growing at only half the Canadian rate, there is a feeling of invasion. Interest rates are 1 to 3 per cent lower in Washington, and land is cheaper, so Canadians will continue to come across the border. One of them is William Wien of Vancouver, who bought a modified A-frame in the Paradise Lakes development near Kendall on the Mount Baker highway. "We've always wanted a place in the woods and a cabin to get away from it all," Wien says. "We finally did and we're spending almost every weekend here." Because Canadians are the majority in the developments of redwood A-frames and boxy ranch houses, they appear not to feel the pressure of the "invasion syndrome." But some of the more vocal local residents say that it's only a matter of time until they do.

Pride is at the center of it, and an uneasy feeling that as the economic balance shifts, other people's conceptions of us change, and ours of them. The realization is not always comfortable. Dr. Gerald F. Rhutan, director of the Canadian studies program at Bellingham's Western Washington State College, notes wryly that "People here are in the process of realizing we are a bedroom suburb of Vancouver. People tended to look at Vancouver as 'the outback,' when it is really more cosmopolitan and developed than Seattle. We are like the Tijuana of the North."

For people who have always thought of their dollar as being worth more than the Canadian dollar, that is tough to swallow. "If you're a store manager," Rhutan says, "you say 'gee, it's nice to have 1,000 Canadians each day.' But store managers don't realize that if you welcome the Canadian's business you become part of the cultural make-up of Canada. The clout in this part of the country rests in Vancouver. We've just got to adjust ourselves, as cities in northern New Jersey adjust to New York City. People can adjust."

CANADIAN OIL AND THE UNITED STATES [4]

Reprinted from *U.S. News & World Report*.

Mr. Minister, if the U. S. should be hit by another Arab embargo, would Canada be able to furnish this country [the United States] more oil and natural gas than it is furnishing at this time?

The answer probably is "Yes." It would depend very much on the supply situation in Canada itself. If as a result of the embargo there was also a shutback in supplies to Canada, we naturally would have to try to meet our own needs first to the best of our ability. But if there was not a shutback, then there would be the possibility of increasing supplies.

I should say that the over-all capability of providing very much more is not very great from Canada. We're about at the maximum of our productive capacity . . . , and therefore we're not talking about any very considerable amount.

How much of these two fuels are . . . flowing from Canada to the U. S.? And is this an increase over past years?

In terms of oil, it's . . . [600,000 to 700,000] barrels a day. It varies from month to month, partly related to season and refinery demand. That represents a descent from about 1.1 million, 1.2 million at the maximum back in 1973.

Going back to a historical period, you were shutting out our oil under the import-restriction program. The minimum, I think, was 500,000 barrels a day several years ago. From that approximately 500,000 barrels a day it worked up to about 1.1 million, and has moved off that peak down again, principally because of the growth in demand in Canada.

[4] From "Canada to U. S. on Oil: 'We'll Meet Our Own Needs First,'" interview with Donald S. Macdonald, Canada's former minister of energy, mines and resources, 1972-1975. *U.S. News & World Report.* 77:39-40+. O. 28, '74.

Our natural-gas exports to the U. S. are about a trillion cubic feet a year.

And that compares to the . . . [24] trillion- . . . [25] trillion total that is used in the U. S.?

Yes.

What are the possibilities of expanding your productive capacity in both areas so that you could increase exports to the United States?

In terms of accessible resources, there are not great possibilities.

The Western Canada sedimentary basin, which is primarily in Alberta, has, by the counts of most of the geological authorities, reached its peak. Most of the major reservoirs have now been probed there. Not only will we not be able to increase it, as our own demand grows the export level will be descending through the balance of this decade. But it will be descending in a fashion which we would, of course, discuss with your government so that it would minimize damage to American purchasers.

In the longer run, the next area of Canadian resources is primarily in the high Arctic, and there are two uncertainties involved there:

The first, exploration, is just now under way. They have identified in some cases some substantial hydrocarbons, but that is still being defined.

And, of course, the second question mark is the construction of pipeline links to bring that down.

Now, it's going to be a matter of policy at that time—and we're talking about the late '70s, the early '80s—before we know how much is going to be coming down, what our own demand is, and whether we'll be able to satisfy your market or not.

Compared with the U. S., Canada seems to be in a relatively fortunate position in that you are not a net importer and presumably will not be for the foreseeable future—

. . . At the rate of demand growth in our own country, we probably will be a net importer in several years' time. [In 1976, Canada became an importer of oil.—Ed.]

. . . When you have to use all of your own supplies and import some more to get by—does that mean nothing will flow south of the border?

It certainly is possible that at some stage, somewhere between the late 1970s and the early '80s, that exports from Canada will have been phased down perhaps to zero or perhaps to an absolute minimum to deal with certain of the northern U. S. refineries which it makes economic sense to serve from Canada. [Canada's official policy is to halt all oil exports by 1983.—Ed.]

Would this be true of gas, also?

It seems less evident with regard to gas.

An Arab leader said . . . that Canadian oil is costing the U. S. more than Arab oil. Is that accurate?

It possibly is true in the case of some Arab oil. For example, spot shipments of oil coming into the U. S. market are lower priced than Canadian oil. What we've been doing in pricing our oil is to consider the long-term contract price of oil coming in from Venezuela and the Persian Gulf. And on this basis, while there is certain softness in the market now and you can get cheaper oil, you must remember that we weren't charging you outrageous prices when there was a shortage at $15 a barrel.

So I think that our Energy Board at least regards this as a just and reasonable price in relation to what other American users have to pay.

Why is it just and reasonable for a neighbor to be charging the same price as the Arabs—a price many Americans regard as highway robbery?

One of the reasons it's just and reasonable is that on other commodities you charge us world prices. So is there any particular reason why Canadians should be selling their oil to the United States for less than Venezuela charges?

Just because you love us—

Well, that's true. But from a purely practical standpoint, we sell to you about the same amount as we buy from overseas. And it would be very difficult to be paying top dollar overseas and giving you a discount.

In other words, you have to import part of your supply at the high price—

Yes. Basically, the market is structured with a mythical line drawn somewhere in Central Canada, and we would import about between . . . [600,000 and 700,000] barrels a day for the Eastern Provinces [Ontario and Quebec], which is, as I said, about what we export to you. So we're roughly in balance in our trade accounts.

Why Price of Gas Is Going Up

. . . Your policy seems to be based on the idea that fuels inevitably are going to become more and more expensive as the years go by. Is that right?

That's right. And we accept the fact that the days of cheap energy are over—if they ever, in true economic terms, did exist. And in this sense natural gas as a premium fuel has been underpriced for regulatory reasons. We should bring it into competitive relationship with other competing fuels.

Does this mean that you feel that the price of Arab oil is a reasonable market price . . . ?

No. I think we would say that the OPEC [Organization of Petroleum Exporting Countries] oil—let's not just single out the Arabs—is probably about $2 over what would be a reasonable price.

Is there a kind of common approach between the United States and Canada on the question of trying to bring down the price of Arab oil?

There has not been. Nor, indeed, has there been a common approach between the U. S. and any of her other Western partners. You may recall that there was an approach attempted through a Washington conference . . . [in the winter of 1973–74] which has not been fully successful, but the time may well have come in which a fresh diplomatic initiative could be made, although I think we would have to face the fact that there would be a number of other issues brought to the table.

Such as?

Primarily economic issues, such as the impact on some of the OPEC states of other cost increases for manufactured goods and food. Behind it all, of course, is the question which was the source of the disruption last year: the Middle East political situation. That's primarily not an OPEC problem so much as an Arab problem.

How big a role does that play in this?

It plays an important role. Obviously the Arab states are as strongly motivated by the use of oil as an instrument in that contest as by using oil as a means of economic development. But when the Venezuelans and the Iranians come to the table, the resolution of those questions is not of primary interest to them.

It is conceivable that in the light of the difficult situation that the world economy finds itself in . . . that it would be possible to negotiate a lower price. But I'm saying equally that these are questions which are of such fundamental importance to the Arab states, they're never going to be very far away from negotiations.

Are you proposing a meeting of the oil-consuming and oil-producing nations at some time in the near future? Is that what you're referring to when you say—

I'm not specifically making a statesman's appeal that we get together under the aegis and the beneficial climate of Canada and do it, and so on. But we certainly would support international initiative in this regard.

Now, on the question of oil pricing, it obviously is in the long-run interest of Canada to have oil priced higher than the price that existed, say, up until September of 1973. It's a little difficult to calculate exactly what the appropriate price is for Arab oil, our tar-sands oil or frontier oil. . . .

In other words, even in knocking $2 or $3 off the current international price, we still think that there's a very viable price for the development of Canadian potential as well as, of course, for the development of your own domestic potential.

A Watchful Eye on Inflation

Would you favor developing your oil sands on a crash basis?

No, I think we have to be very concerned about that with a relatively smaller economy. The principal concern my colleague, the minister of finance, has is the inflationary impact of doing major construction projects right on top of each other rather than timing them. And, of course, there is the impact on our balance of payments, if we're going to be raising substantial sums on foreign markets or wherever. We have to be concerned about the impact on the external value of the Canadian dollar.

We went through this in the '50s, when the Canadian dollar went to a premium of about 7 cents over the American dollar, because of the continued inflow of investment into Canada at that time. And this, of course, creates competitive problems for Canadian secondary industry. One of the national ambitions is to move away from the primary, unprocessed materials to a more highly processed stage for natural commodities, and, of course, to move into secondary manufacture.

So any effect on the external value of the Canadian dollar which sets us at a competitive disadvantage works against one of the objectives of Canadian economic policy.

Mr. Minister, whatever happened to the continental energy policy that the United States and Canada were discussing . . . [in 1973]? Has that been replaced by a Canada-first policy?

We always felt that continental energy policy amounted to this: We would bring to the table our resources and you'd bring to the table your shortages.

In many ways it is not in our national interest to do this. I think that in specific cases, on an *ad hoc* basis, that we would be negotiating arrangements, but that we really wouldn't give up our freedom of decision by a comprehensive umbrella treaty saying, "O.K., from now on these resources are to be planned bilaterally."

Are you saying that the U. S. is being selfish and unrealistic in expecting the rest of the world to meet its energy shortage at a price that it considers reasonable?

No, I wouldn't use those words. After all, we're looking after our interests and you're going to look after yours. We acknowledge that.

I'm saying that we don't regard it as being in our interests to, in effect, put our resources under the umbrella of a major accord of that kind. On individual resource projects the arrangements will be negotiated. But we'd like to keep our freedom of choice open, and we would forfeit that freedom of choice if there was a continental energy policy.

I'd have to say one other thing. . . . we are very substantially net importers from you of Appalachian coal for metallurgical and steam-coal reasons in Ontario. The mineral exchange is not all one way. Indeed, on two very critical commodities—Appalachian coal and phosphate rock—Canada is the customer of the U. S. So that we have an interest over a period of time in keeping the channels of trade open.

Is the U. S. gouging you for those?

Oh, the price has increased . . . but we're not complaining.

When you extend your pipelines into Eastern Canada, will that in turn divert some of the Alberta crude from the U. S. market into the Canadian market?

In due course it will. A major diversion, of course, will occur because of an American decision. Canadian oil will be backed out of the West Coast market when Alaskan oil starts coming in. But in due course the extension of pipelines to Montreal will reduce the ability of the Canadian reservoir to satisfy some part of the American market.

Exploding "a Pollyanna Feeling"

Then all you have for the U. S. is bad news—

It's a realistic viewpoint of where we stand. There has

been a kind of Pollyanna feeling in both of our countries that everything is going to work out all right—that we had near-inexhaustible resources and that there were no problems. In fact, we're trying to be more realistic with our own people and saying that "not only should you be paying a lot more than you are right now, but you ought to be concerned about supplies."

Most Americans think that Canadians have no energy problem. You didn't have lineups at gas stations . . . [during OPEC's 1973-1974 winter oil embargo] or even invoke the kind of voluntary conservation measures—

We engaged in certain hortatory measures to persuade people to take less out of the market. We were not subject to a total embargo, but we were subject to the results of the progressive production shutbacks by the Arab states.

What do you think about some sort of mandatory conservation program?

We think its's desirable from a national standpoint. We have an Office of Energy Conservation which is inclined to direct itself more to the longer-run factors of, for example, in a cold climate, better insulation, more-efficient use. But I think there is some considerable scope in Canada for improving the efficiency of industrial energy use. If there is a tendency within the American auto industry to move to more-efficient use of gasoline, then this, of course, will have an impact on us.

But are you going to be relying primarily on higher prices to encourage people to be less wasteful?

The Government controls the wholesale price in Canada, and . . . by progressive increases in price we're achieving many of the same things that the U. S. would achieve by increasing fuel taxes.

Both from the standpoint of the ultimate exhaustion of our available resources and from the international-responsibility standpoint, we agree with the general principle we should try to get a more economic use of the wasted gasoline.

As Fear of Depression Mounts

There are widespread fears of a worldwide depression triggered by the inability of the consumer countries to pay for their oil imports. In your view, how should this problem be tackled?

I'm afraid I don't have a simple answer to it. I think it would be of some assistance, of course, to at least reduce the dimensions of the problem by knocking a couple of dollars off the price. But you would then still have a substantial transfer of real income from the developed nations to some of the developing countries.

I would think that, dealing with one aspect of the problem, that we could expect the OPEC countries to assume a greater share than they have heretofore for economic assistance to the less-developed countries who are not themselves oil producers. But, if there's going to be a shift in real income, then some part of that shift should be used to meet the problems of other less-developed countries.

Do you see this as temporary, or is it a new problem that we're going to have to live with for a very long time?

I can't think of any reason why it will go away, except possibly for some developed countries like yours and mine which, over a period time, will be able to develop alternative energy sources.

Some, such as the United Kingdom—because of the development of the North Sea [oil fields], of course—are going to move into a position where they'll be less dependent on it. But others again, like Germany, France, Italy and Japan, are going to continue to have a difficult situation in this regard.

What does that mean? Are they going to have to take a declining standard of living or go into heavy debt on a very-long-term basis?

Unless some means is found of handling the problem, inevitably, over time, real incomes will drop because the terms of trade have shifted against them.

And as to the financial means of managing this, I'm afraid I don't have a suggestion.

AN ALASKAN-CANADIAN PIPELINE? [5]

The first pipeline out of Alaska's North Slope prompted nearly five years of environmental squabbling and a delay-induced, 755% cost overrun. Nor is the controversy over. When it is completed next summer [1977], some critics charge, the $7.7 billion line will do nothing but create unmanageable surpluses of crude oil on the U.S. West Coast.

Now, a second Alaskan pipeline is in the works. It will transport natural gas instead of oil and could be even more costly than the first line. No pipe has been laid, because backers of three separate proposals for the gas line are still vying for regulatory approval. Yet there's already a controversy brewing; the environment, patriotism and money are just a few of the issues in dispute.

This time around, however, there are indications that an Alaskan gas pipeline crossing Canada as well might be built without the delays, if not the criticism, encountered by the oil pipeline. That is because the U.S. and Canadian governments are quietly edging toward a partnership effort, perhaps deciding by as early as next spring [1977] to approve one of the three gas pipeline proposals. Should they do so, the impact could be enormous, involving these governments far beyond mere regulatory review.

For one thing, because of the huge sums at stake, both nations are likely to provide financial guarantees to any of the proposed gas pipelines they might decide to back. Opposition by environmental and other groups could also be limited; both Canadian law and a recently-passed U.S. bill sharply narrow the types of objections that can be raised against a second Alaskan pipeline. And finally, a joint U.S.-

[5] From "Another Alaskan Pipeline Is in the Works as the U.S., Canada, Mull a Joint Venture," by Tim Metz, a staff reporter. Wall Street Journal. p 42. O. 18, '76. Reprinted with permission of The Wall Street Journal © 1976 Dow Jones & Company, Inc. All Rights Reserved.

Canadian venture would dash the hopes of one of the gas-line applicants, a unit of El Paso Co., that has excluded Canadian participation in its own $7.9 billion proposal.

Opting for Arctic Gas

Currently, both governments appear to be favoring the most costly proposal, the Arctic Gas Project, which some say would involve outlays of $9 billion to $10 billion. Sponsored by a consortium of 15 U.S. and Canadian gas transmission and other energy companies, the project proposes to move both Alaskan North Slope and Canadian Mackenzie Delta gas across Canada t market through the same pipeline.

"If we had to nake our decision tomorrow, there's no question we'd op' for Arctic Gas," confides a Canadian government source lose to the deliberations. "But if you print that, I'll have to deny it," he adds. A spokesman for the U.S Federal Power Commission refuses to say if the Arctic Gas Project has the inside track at that agency. Recently, however, some FPC staff members have publicly stated they see advantages in certain aspects of the Arctic Gas proposal.

There's still heavy competition from the $4.6 billion-plus Alcan proposal, another Alaska-Canada routed pipeline sponsored by Alberta Natural Gas Co. and Westcoast Transmission Co., both Canadian firms, and by the Salt Lake City-based Northwest Pipeline Corp. unit of Northwest Energy Co. Initially, the Alcan proposal didn't include any provision for transporting Canadian gas; now, its backers say they would agree to connect their line to another proposed pipeline running south from the Mackenzie Delta.

Although no assurance can be made that the U.S. and Canada will agree on which project to back, there is at least a timetable for a decision. Minutes before its recent adjournment, the U.S. Congress passed a bill requiring the FPC to recommend one of the three gas pipeline proposals to the President, who in turn must make a final choice before the end of . . . [1977]. The bill, which President Ford is expected to sign, also limits court challenges of the type used by environmental groups to delay the Alaskan oil line. [President Ford signed the bill in 1976.—Ed.]

Shortages Predicted

Both countries have ample incentive to form a successful partnership. Canada's National Energy Board, for instance, estimates that unless arctic reserves are tapped, Canada's gas demand will begin exceeding its domestic supply by the early 1980s. That would aggravate worsening gas shortages in the U.S. because the Canadians, who currently supply up to three-quarters of the gas used in some U.S. border states, have promised to cut these exports whenever shortages develop at home.

The Arctic Gas Project, filed with the FPC over two years ago, proposes to avert this future dilemma by taking gas from the North Slope and the nearby Mackenzie Delta and transporting it to a spot in Alberta near the U.S. border. At this point, the system would split, one leg delivering gas to Pacific markets and another servicing Midwest and Eastern customers in both countries.

A major criticism of the Arctic Gas Project proposal is that it re-opens the whole question of the impact of any pipeline system on the delicate environment found in arctic regions. Taking advantage of these concerns, backers of the Alcan gas line came forward earlier this year with their proposal: A pipeline following the route of the Alaskan oil line to a point south of Fairbanks, then turning east to connect with existing gas lines in British Columbia and Alberta that already cross into the U.S.

U.S. environmentalists back the Alcan proposal because much of its route follows the existing right-of-way not only of the oil line but also that of the Alaska-Canada highway. "It is this fact alone that causes every environmental group I know of in this country to oppose the Arctic Gas route with all the resources we have," says Brock Evans, director of the Sierra Club's Washington office.

Pleasing Canada

Some Canadian nationalists also like the Alcan proposal because of its comparatively lower $4.6 billion capital costs. They assert that Canadian money markets aren't up to the financing requirements of the Arctic Gas Project, and so "the result would be a massive, unwanted influx of foreign funds," says Daryl Logan, a spokesman for the Committee for an Independent Canada, a group that believes foreigners exert too much control over Canadian business assets. "The Alcan proposal would seem to be more realistic," he adds.

Understandably galled by the newcomer, Arctic Gas Project officials went on the offensive, pointing out they had already spent $120 million on environmental and engineering studies and tests. They also complained to Canadian regulators that the Alcan proposal failed to provide any means of transporting Canada's arctic gas reserves to market.

In response to this latter charge, Alcan backers quickly let it be known that they would combine their system with a previously-proposed, Canadian pipeline to the Mackenzie Delta. That may have been a mistake. Some critics, including a few FPC staff members, now suggest that this combination would add billions to the Alcan line's capital costs, creating a system less efficient and more costly to operate than the Arctic Gas Project.

It is possible, of course, that neither Alcan nor Arctic Gas will be chosen. Regional squabbles over pipeline routes, now intensifying, could produce a stalemate in the U.S., where any pipeline decision by the President would still be subject to congressional approval. And in Canada, all-Canadian pipelines linking either the Mackenzie Delta or the Arctic Islands with southern markets are still preferred by many of that nation's vocal nationalists. In the absence of agreement on Arctic Gas or Alcan, El Paso's proposal, filed during a period of uneasiness over rising Canadian nationalism and calling for an all-U.S., combination pipeline and ocean tanker delivery system, would be the only remaining alternative for transporting Alaskan gas.

MANAGING INFLATION [6]

Last week [in October 1976] saw the first anniversary of an exceptional effort by perhaps the world's most gifted leader to put the lid on inflation. A year ago Thursday [on October 23, 1975], here in Canada, Prime Minister Pierre Elliott Trudeau initiated a long-term program to wean this country away from the underlying inflationary bias that has beset so many industrialized nations.

The results, so far, suggest modest progress. "We've brought down inflationary expectations," Mr. Trudeau said in an interview with me. But he also acknowledged that he had paid a "pretty heavy price" in personal popularity and national unity.

The setting for the policy initiated by Trudeau was a particularly noxious and stubborn inflation. Price increases were running at 11.6 per cent annually. Canada had not suffered the disciplinary shock of the oil shortage and price rise of 1973, for Canadians believed—wrongly, it has turned out—they were rich in oil and gas reserves. Moreover, these price increases were being chiefly forced by high wage demands from the type of unions most difficult to manage—the unions of public service employees.

In 1975 government workers in Canada won average wage increases of over 22 per cent, and their demands were immediately spread to other sectors of the economy. As preparations for the 1976 wage bargaining began last fall [1975], unions were asking for increases of as much as 100 per cent.

In these conditions, Trudeau felt impelled to get at the underlying causes of inflation. He avoided the usual, easy gesture of a 90-day freeze. Although he had won reelection

[6] From "An Inflationary Lesson from Canada," by Joseph Kraft, columnist. Washington *Post.* p A-19. O. 19, '76. Joseph Kraft, Copyright © 1976, Field Enterprises Inc., reproduced through the courtesy of Field Newspaper Syndicate.

in 1974 by campaigning against controls. he put into effect
a three-year program built around an Anti-Inflation Board,
empowered to review and roll back price and wage rises.

In explaining the three-year program, Trudeau expresses
the deep seriousness of his effort. He told me:

"We wanted people to realize they couldn't look past the
control period and figure out how to catch up when the 90
days were over. We wanted them to realize there had to be
some change in behavior and in institutions. We wanted
them to see that the expectations of continually increasing
wealth no longer applied."

The most immediate consequence of the policy has been
a decline in the rate of price increases from 11.6 to 6.5 per
cent annually. Companies acknowledge that the sheer com-
plexity of dealing with the Anti-Inflation Board has deterred
some price rises. Wage settlements have declined from a 15
per cent annual increase to a 9 per cent rise this year.

Since the decline in inflation has outpaced the decline
in wages, workers are actually better off. They don't have
to keep chasing their tails anymore in the classic inflationary
cycle. "Nobody even remembers what they were asking last
year," Trudeau says in what is perhaps his proudest boast.

But the controls have generated strong opposition from
labor, which last week called a partially successful general
strike, and business. The prime minister has lost standing
because of his flip-flop on controls. In the Gallup poll, his
Liberal party which enjoyed a 12-point lead over the opposition Tories last February now trails by 11 points.

The general weakening of the government has put into
question Trudeau's most impressive achievement—the apparent settlement of the struggle between French-speaking
Quebec and the English-speaking rest of the country by
making both languages official throughout Canada. In western Canada especially now, there is criticism of Trudeau's
bias toward Quebec. [In Quebec, too, there is discontent, as
evidenced by the November 1976 provincial elections in
which separatist Parti Québécois leader René Lévesque and

his party were swept into office in a landslide victory.—Ed.]

In these conditions, controls can not go on forever. But before lifting them, Trudeau is determined to internalize the restraints that are now imposed by government.

"The problem of industrial society today," he says, "is to accept some kind of restraint, some kind of discipline. We're trying to get Canadians to ask how will discipline and restraint be maintained when controls are gone?"

The lesson for all other countries, including the United States, is unmistakable. It is that weaning industrial societies away from constantly rising expectations is an extremely difficult task, requiring, as Trudeau put it, "the highest degree of understanding, skill and commitment." No one can look at the Canadian experience and be optimistic about the rest of the world where presidents and prime ministers are so much less intelligent and so much less willing to sacrifice popularity to principle than Trudeau.

V. CANADA'S FOREIGN RELATIONS

EDITOR'S INTRODUCTION

Canada's external relations are as complex and far-reaching as are those of the United States. And although many Americans choose to ignore the fact, Canada's foreign relations can no longer be considered a mirror image of our own. It is the foreign policy of Canada—largely determined now by its growing nationalist beliefs—that is the subject of the articles in this section.

Indeed, Canadian-American relations in 1976 can be characterized as being in a transitional stage, with the emphasis placed on more Canadian independence and less American influence. This situation is dealt with in a staff report of the Canadian-American Committee, a joint Canadian-American-sponsored organization. The recent cooling in relations between the two countries is next described in an interview with Gerson Yalowitz, former Ottawa bureau chief of *U.S. News & World Report*.

Then follows a selection which provides a brief description of Canada's buildup of its armed forces. The two concluding articles present a picture of Canada's relations with two areas of the world: Western Europe and the Third World, those nonaligned nations whose overall economic instability belies their enormous collective political influence.

CANADA-U.S. RELATIONS IN TRANSITION [1]

The Canada-U.S. relationship is in a state of transition. Old issues fester, and complicated new problems emerge

[1] From *A Time of Difficult Transitions: Canada-U.S. Relations in 1976*, a staff report of the Canadian-American Committee. C. D. Howe Research Institute. 2060 Sun Life Bldg. Montreal, Que. H3B 2X7. Canada; National Planning Association. 1606 New Hampshire Ave. N.W. Washington, DC 20009. '76. p 1-7, 52-4.

with disturbing regularity. Thus far, the close formal and informal ties that link the two nations and the underlying bilateral goodwill that exists among the majority of people on both sides of the border have prevented a serious rupture in the relationship. But the current situation can best be described as tense, with little prospect for a near-term resolution of fundamental issues that are straining the relationship from many directions.

The purpose of this report is to review some of the major developments of the past few years that have shaped the current state of the bilateral relationship and to examine the most likely near-term trends and issues in that relationship. In this introduction the theme of difficult transitions is developed and related to a variety of recent bilateral issues. . . .

Progressively closer links between Canada and the United States since World War II evolved from government policy decisions and, to a much greater degree, from private individuals responding to opportunities and incentives created by natural market forces. As this process continued, Canada's ability to sustain a separate identity from the United States was perceived as a problem by an increasing number of Canadians. The government of Prime Minister [Pierre Elliott] Trudeau has sought to mobilize this concern into support for policies that would override the integrative tendencies of natural market forces.

Canadian policies having a bearing on the bilateral relationship are based, at least implicitly, on two hypotheses, neither of which has been subjected to careful research. First, it is assumed that closer economic integration between Canada and the United States necessarily implies greater integration in other areas—cultural, social, and especially political. (Given the asymmetry in the size of the two economies and populations, it is further assumed that the United States would dominate this integrative process.) Second, there is an assumption either that policies aimed at overriding natural market forces will not result in significant costs to the Canadian economy or, if they do, that these costs will be accepted by the majority of Canadians.

In the economic sphere, Canadian policies are being directed towards the objectives of greater diversity in trade relationships, increased ownership and control of domestic economic activity, and improved balance in the sources of domestic economic growth. Trade diversity is being sought through a program of expanding contacts and bilateral undertakings with nations throughout the world, with the most notable, and as yet still very vague, example being Canada's . . . "contractual link" with the European Community. Foreign investment in the form of acquisitions of enterprises in Canada and of expansion by foreign-owned firms into new lines of activity in Canada is being screened by the Foreign Investment Review Agency, established in 1974, to ensure "significant benefits" for Canada. More "balanced" growth is a concept that has not been defined precisely for policy purposes but that essentially means industrial and regional diversity and an upgrading of domestic capacities in a broad range of economic activities. It is the objective of efforts to promote further processing of Canadian resources prior to export; regional and industrial incentive programs; government purchases of equipment from foreign suppliers that are tied to provisions for subcontracting in Canada; and measures to strengthen Canadian capabilities in areas covering such diverse industries as publishing, finance, advertising, film-making, etc.

The Role of "Cultural Nationalism"

There are non-economic dimensions to many of these Canadian policy initiatives. "Cultural nationalism," for example, is one of these dimensions that has emerged in recent actions affecting *Time/Canada* and the broadcasting of television programs originating from U.S. stations over Canadian cable systems. In both instances, one of the major stated objectives was to improve Canadian potential in the cultural field by increasing the flow of domestic advertising expenditures to Canadian enterprises. In the case of *Time/Canada,* a long-standing exemption to Canada's tax provisions, which had allowed Canadian firms' advertising in *Time*'s Canadian edition as a business expense, was removed early in 1976, resulting in the termination of this special edition. Canadian cable television operators in some areas are now required to delete commercial segments of programs taken off the air from the United States with the objective of diverting the current outflow of advertising dollars away from U.S. border stations. Cultural objectives also underline Canadian-content requirements for domestic radio and television broadcasts and pressures to require cinema chains to devote a certain portion of the year to the showing of Canadian-made films.

Other important developments redirecting the bilateral relationship are even more complex. At one level, provincial initiatives in Canada may be redirecting the relationship more rapidly, or in very different directions, than the federal government would wish to see. Examples that have brought some embarrassment to the federal government include the announcement by the Saskatchewan government that it intends to take over part of that province's potash industry, much of which is currently developed by private, foreign-owned firms, and the decision of the British Columbia government in 1974 to suspend natural gas shipments to Washington state under long-term contract without prorationing between domestic and foreign customers.

At a much broader level, changes in international relations are creating a new environment within which decisions by both countries concerning the bilateral relationship must be made and assessed. "Cold War" confrontations have gradually given way to new issues in international relations based more on economic rivalry than on strategic alignments. This environment, in which issues of "fairness" in national and regional economic policies have taken on a greater importance, shapes the perceptions of many people in the United States concerning Canadian initiatives to redirect the relationship.

The U.S. government appears willing to accept Canada's longer-term objectives for the bilateral relationship as inevitable and even understandable. Despite signs of strain over specific "irritants" and despite calls by some Americans for retaliatory action when Canadian measures have been perceived as harmful to U.S. interests, the U.S. government has stressed the importance of consultation rather than to threaten countermeasures. Still, the United States had contributed, and may even have sparked, the redirection exercise. It has refused in recent years to differentiate its policies to accommodate Canada's claims for special treatment with respect to the temporary import surcharge imposed in mid-1971 and the DISC [Domestic International Sales Corporations] tax legislation passed later that year; and it adopted a strict interpretation of U.S. law regarding countervailing duties when it imposed a modest penalty on exports of Michelin tires from Canada to the United States on the grounds that these exports received an unfair "bounty or grant" in the form of inducements to production from the federal and provincial governments.

Even though both governments continue to claim that bilateral relations are essentially cooperative and friendly, issues are accumulating during a transitional process that both sides would like to see take place gradually and with as little hostility as possible. Three types of problems illustrate the difficulties inherent in this longer-term transition.

First, because the Canadian government is attempting to override natural market forces tending to advance the degree of North American integration, its policies must be interventionist. The U.S. government, in contrast, at least under Presidents Nixon and Ford, . . . supported a philosophy that is far more market-oriented. (It is indicative of differences in economic philosophies that Mr. Ford . . . [was] pressing for "deregulation" of many government controls at the same time that Mr. Trudeau . . . [was] indicating that new forms of long-term government controls may be necessary following the current wage and price measures, now scheduled for removal at the end of 1978.) An example of the kinds of issues that can arise from different attitudes towards market forces is provided by the Automotive Agreement, where negotiations for changes in its terms have reached an apparent impasse because the U.S. position is based on the goal of greater market freedom whereas the Canadian position is to seek new undertakings to regulate the market. Other types of issues in this area are illustrated by the recent case of Canadian import quotas on eggs.

Second, there is a fine line between upgrading a nation's capabilities, on the one hand, and protectionism, on the other. That line is determined as much by perception as by fact. There are currently serious challenges in the international economic system to trade liberalization, "fair" trade, and multilateralism. The United States, as one of the major proponents of an open world trading system, is being watched closely by other nations not only in terms of its own actions but also in terms of the principles it adopts in its trade relations with other nations, including Canada.

Third, there has been a move away from bilateral policy initiatives of the type that create potential advantages to both sides (the Automotive Agreement would be an example of such an initiative, as would the Defence-Production-Sharing Agreement; energy swaps would be a possible example for the future). Issues are now being examined separately from one another, and it is virtually impossible politically for the Canadian government to appear to be giving up something to the United States, even if in return for a broader agreement bringing greater benefits. It is unrealistic to think that issues can continue to accumulate in which Canada's perceived gains are achieved at the expense of someone in the United States (as in the cases of *Time/Canada*, cable television, oil export cutbacks, the potash takeover, etc.) without resentment mounting and pressures for retaliatory actions by the U.S. government increasing.

Even with the best of intentions and with basic understanding between the two governments, issues of the sort raised here make difficult the longer-term transition now taking place as a result of Canadian attempts to redirect the relationship.

Process of Economic Recovery

The outlook for bilateral relations over the next few years is likely to be affected significantly by the process of recovery from the sharp economic downturn of 1974–75. Both countries face difficult transitions from high inflation and high unemployment to reasonably full employment with improved price stability, but at the present time the tasks facing Canada appear to be the more difficult. Because the economic downturn was less severe in Canada than in the United States, the above-average productivity gains that normally accompany an economic recovery will be harder to achieve in Canada; while Canada's trade performance can be expected to improve (especially in the automotive and resource sectors) as the U.S. and other major economies pick up, its current account balance is likely to remain in substantial deficit this year and probably next; and the full consequences of changes in compartive wage costs, with Canada's rising faster than those in the United States, may take several years to unfold.

The exchange rate is presenting Canada with some particularly perplexing problems. As of the early spring of 1976, the Canadian dollar was trading at a modest premium in relation to the U.S. dollar in the spot (for immediate delivery) market, representing an appreciation of nearly 10 percent in relation to the U.S. dollar since early 1970, just prior to the time it was allowed to "float." Yet over this same period, there was a deterioration in Canada's overall trade account of nearly $3 billion. Furthermore, the "gap" between Canadian and U.S. manufacturing wages has essentially been eliminated, while a substantial productivity differential remains, putting Canada in a less competitive position.

High interest rates in Canada are encouraging capital inflows into Canada and keeping the exchange rate for the Canadian dollar strong. In the short run, at least, capital inflows will continue to be necessary to finance Canada's current account deficit, even if the exchange rate should fall. (It takes time for a lower exchange rate to show up in an improved trade performance.) These capital inflows, when they come in the form of purchases of Canadian debt, create future interest obligations on a fixed schedule, and these obligations have to be met by either higher foreign exchange earnings or additional borrowing. To complicate matters further, even if the Canadian dollar were to fall in value, import prices paid by Canadians would rise, adding to future inflationary problems.

Looking at the near-term economic outlook in Canada, then, it is reasonable to expect some combination of the following to occur:

☐ The need to sustain capital inflows will allow limited scope for independent Canadian monetary policy. Furthermore, equity capital may have to be sought, or at least not rejected, both to meet capital financing needs and to relieve the pressure from mounting fixed commitments for debt servicing.

☐ Canada will have to seek whatever export markets can be found, and this will probably mean a continuing reliance of primary-product exports, with manufacturing exports having to struggle to overcome comparative cost handicaps.

☐ The value of the Canadian dollar will eventually come under downward pressure if interest rates begin to decline relative to those in the United States and abroad. It will be difficult to determine what new level for the exchange rate would be appropriate until the impact of differences in recent Canadian and U.S. economic performance works itself out. . . .

It should be noted that some of the basic objectives Canada is seeking to achieve through its attempts to redirect the relationship are going to be difficult to realize because of the problems associated with the process of economic recovery outlined above. A major uncertainty at the present time concerns how the Canadian government will respond to this situation.

Decisions Affecting Shared Resources

Many of the most important issues in Canadian-American relations concern the use of resources that are shared. These include rivers that flow across the boundary and migratory fish and fowl. On occasion these issues emerge as major news items—such as the Garrison Diversion Project in North Dakota, which is anticipated to affect water quality of the Souris River in Canada adversely, and the proposal to raise the water level behind the Ross Dam in Washington state, flooding land in the Skagit Valley in Canada—but both countries have fully recognized their common interests and mutual obligations in these issues. Well-tried procedures have been adopted for settling disputes, with a leading role being played by the International Joint Commission, an advisory and research group appointed by both countries but with a responsibility for independence. . . .

The Near-Term Outlook

Many of the issues examined in this report arise from developments that extend far beyond the context of Canada-U.S. relations. Inflation, recession, and energy challenges are global in their scope and impact, and an effective resolution of the problems they have created must be sought through international means based on sound domestic policies. Transitions have been, and continue to be, made in response to important changes in the economic, political, and social environment facing the international community, but it would be premature to conclude that the adjustments in expectations and actions required to restore reasonable stability will be forthcoming. Inflationary pressures persist, unemployment remains unacceptably high, and long-term approaches to meeting energy needs are lacking.

The immediate future, however, is likely to be a distinct improvement over the recent past. Economic growth has begun to accelerate, paced by a solid recovery in the United States; inflation rates in almost all industrialized countries have improved considerably from a year ago; and world oil prices and supplies appear to have stabilized. Global recession has created, at a very high cost, a temporary "breathing space" within which effective policies for the future can be devised and implemented. Whether or not this time will be used wisely remains an open question, with the viability of existing economic and political systems potentially hanging in the balance.

Moving from the global to the bilateral, an improved economic outlook should contribute positively to several problem areas in Canada-U.S. relations. Canada's automotive trade deficit with the United States, for example, should be reduced significantly with a continuation of the kind of improved U.S. sales performance for North American vehicles registered in recent months. At a more general level, Canada has traditionally benefited from the demand for imports generated in an expansion phase of the U.S. business cycle. Even so, production costs in Canada have risen faster than in the United States for several years, and this situation creates the need for adjustments in coming months and years that will be difficult but essential if Canada is to meet its economic objectives and potential.

New U.S.-Canadian Policy Directions

It would be shortsighted, however, to focus exclusively on the near-term economic aspects of the bilateral relationship. Certain major trends predate the global economic disturbances of the past few years. These trends can be summarized by reviewing two themes. . . .

The first theme is that both Canada and the United States are embarking upon new policy directions in response to a variety of domestic and international pressures and imperatives. In the case of the United States, new international policy directions have been necessitated by, and taken in response to, changes in that country's relative role and power in global economic and political relations. The impact of these new policy directions on Canada was not the primary consideration in the United States, but Canada has nevertheless been forced to take initiatives on its own as a defensive reaction.

But Canada's new policy initiatives go beyond strictly defensive responses. A clear trend has emerged in which Canada has asserted itself not only to reduce a perceived "vulnerability" to the United States but to carve out a more distinct Canadian "identity" in economic, cultural, and foreign affairs. These initiatives, which in a number of instances have appeared to outsiders to border on protectionism, have come as often from provincial governments as from the federal government. They have also risen largely from concerns that are judged important by a large number of Canadians and that have been recognized as such by the U.S. government. Still, the speed and scope of these initiatives threaten to create a "backlash" among an increasing number of U.S. citizens, and one is tempted to ask whether Canada has given sufficient attention to the distinction between what is politically desirable in the short run and what is economically necessary in the long run. At some point a danger will arise that, by placing the highest priority on too many objectives at one time, the capacity for bilateral cooperation will be exceeded. If the Canada-U.S. relationship is to remain "unique," this danger point must be avoided.

A second theme is that the momentum for positive, forward-looking bilateral agreements between Canada and the United States appears to be spent, at least for the present. Attention has been focused in both countries on explanations of why bilateral policy issues have emerged, but suggestions as to how to resolve these issues are now too often either lacking or put forward hesitantly and defensively. This situation may be the result of a concern that suggestions for cooperative approaches either will be misinterpreted as "continentalist" in Canada or will otherwise offend national sensitivities in either country.

The past several years have seen, at best, a holding action

in the bilateral relationship. Over the next two years or so, Canada and the United States will face new pressures to determine whether a cooperative accommodation to changing domestic and international circumstances can be achieved. Areas where mutually advantageous accommodation might be reached are being clarified. To cite two examples: it is increasingly recognized that both countries face essentially similar energy challenges, and the possible economies from coordinated transportation facilities would make a contribution to meeting these challenges; and the key role of investment in generating non-inflationary growth is creating a new awareness of the potential costs of artificial barriers to investment flows across the border in both directions.

Commentators in Canada-U.S. relations seem to have a compulsion to make sweeping generalities about the state of the overall relationship as being either "good" or "bad" at a particular point in time. The conclusion to be drawn from this report is that broad generalizations of this sort are neither particularly informative nor appropriate. Difficult transitions, often leading to bilateral frictions, are a fact of the contemporary scene. The fundamental question is whether Canada and the United States will continue to perceive the advantages to their own self-interests in approaching these frictions in a spirit of cooperation in keeping with a relationship that is unique by circumstance, if not always by choice.

WHY FRIENDSHIP HAS COOLED BETWEEN THE UNITED STATES AND CANADA [2]

Reprinted from *U.S. News & World Report.*

There's an impression growing in the U.S. that Canada is turning anti-American. Based on your three years of traveling in Canada, do you feel such a reaction is warranted?

[2] An interview with Gerson Yalowitz, former *U.S. News & World Report* bureau chief in Ottawa. *U.S. News & World Report.* 81:69-70+. O. 18, '76.

It isn't fair to say that Government policy is explicitly anti-American—although some Cabinet ministers may be.

What's happening is that Canada, like many other countries, is becoming more and more nationalistic. And given the tremendous U.S. influence and presence, any "Canada First" actions are bound to affect U.S. interests more than most others.

There is a strident body of Canadians who advocate policies aimed solely at American interests, but it is clearly in the minority. Canada has chafed under American economic, political and cultural domination for years. Now Ottawa appears to be doing everything it can to end this domination—and end it all at once.

What about Americans as individuals? Are they as welcome now as they were three years ago?

At a person-to-person level, the welcome mat is as wide as ever for Americans, especially tourists. I think most Canadians genuinely like their American neighbors despite the "ugly American" cracks you hear.

But if you're talking about Americans who come to Canada seeking positions as college professors or doctors, or those wanting to buy a vacation cottage in prime recreation areas, which drives land prices up, then it's a different story. A lot of Americans in those categories are already here, and many Canadians would prefer that others like them stay at home.

Have there been anti-American demonstrations in Canada?

Not really—not since the end of the Vietnam war. "Go Home Yankee" news sheets pop up occasionally, and one hears boos and hisses at the movies when typically American activities or attitudes appear on the screen.

An interesting point is that the greatest evidence of anti-Americanism is found in academic circles and in the media. But even there it's pretty tame stuff compared with the way Americans are treated in publications in other countries.

Once in a while Canadians will mass to protest certain United States decisions, such as the building of the U.S.

Trident [submarine] base in Washington State south of Vancouver. But you hear little bitter invective at their rallies.

Canadians and Americans travel across the border with almost complete freedom, and neither country keeps troops there. Yet relations now are officially characterized as "unique" rather than "special." What does that mean?

Special, unique or whatever, the American-Canadian relationship boils down to this reality: No two countries in the world have ties as close, deep and entangled. Language, life styles, values, living standards are basically the same. Trade tops 42 billion dollars a year. Cross-border visits run over 70 million a year. There's hardly a Canadian without a relative or close friend living in the States. And that 5,000-mile border must be the longest undefended border in the world.

Until the early 1970s, "special relationship" was the label applied to all these ties. But many Canadians thought the phrase implied a lackey-master relationship, with Ottawa in the subservient position. Washington, for its part, had become accustomed to officials dropping down from Ottawa to appeal for "special consideration" when a U.S. policy threatened to affect Canadian interests.

So when Prime Minister [Pierre Elliott] Trudeau started to lead Canada out of the American shadow by carving a "separate identity" for his country, many felt the "special" label had to go. Washington was agreeable, but also insisted that "special consideration" should also disappear.

But the reality was still there—the common values and language, the peaceful border. As a Canadian politician put it several years ago: "Like it or not, the Americans are our best friends." So wordsmiths came up with the phrase "unique" to describe the U.S.-Canada affinity.

Does Canada have any real grievances against the United States?

Basically, citizens of any country resent domination by another, and pervasive American influence is a fact of life in Canada.

Beyond that, Canadians complain that Americans know

little about Canada—and care even less. They get furious when Americans say, "You're the same as we are," or when U.S. officials refer to Mr. Trudeau as "President of Canada."

Americans in general do take Canadians for granted, and that's probably a big reason why there's a sense of "betrayal" in the U.S. when Ottawa does something that Americans don't like.

What Grievances Does the United States Hold?

What about the other side of the coin? How genuine are the grievances held by the United States—or by the American people in general—against Canada?

One of the main grievances Americans should have—although Washington keeps pretty quiet about it—is the "free ride" Canada gets on defense.

Ottawa talks about the country's huge size and its lack of enemies. But without the American military machine comfortably available—in the Western Hemisphere and in Europe—Canada certainly would have to shell out more to safeguard its vital interests.

Energy is another potential grievance. Canada probably will not honor its long-term contracts to supply gas to American customers, and when the cuts come, there will be sparks. Even Canadian officials tell you that privately.

As Canadian needs increase—at present Canada exports over 40 per cent of its gas production to the U.S.—pressure is going to mount to turn down the tap. Will the cuts be balanced, with both Canadians and Americans sharing the shortfall equally? Don't bet on it.

What about energy-swapping arrangements?

That's likely. In fact, some oil swaps already have been concluded. Swapping makes economic as well as common sense. In some cases, U.S. Midwest refineries are geared to handle only Canadian crude, and changeovers would be costly. Some Canadian heavy-oil producers have only the U.S. market. So, given Ottawa's decision to halt all oil exports by 1983, a trade-off would benefit both sides.

Delivering Alaskan oil to British Columbia on the West Coast in return for continued Canadian shipments to the Midwest would make good sense—depending on price. If the cost of Alaskan crude goes through the roof, it will be hard to convince Canadians to buy it in preference to cheaper Mideast, African or Latin-American oil.

Is there worry over interrupting the flow of gas and oil?

A pipeline treaty has been signed—but not yet ratified—providing protection for oil and gas flowing through each other's territory. It aims to prevent such things as interruptions of delivery or discriminatory taxation.

There is some concern on the U.S. side about how binding the agreement would be on the provincial governments and actions they might take. At any rate, even the treaty would not prevent a price hike or cutback in the export of oil and gas by either country.

Why is Ottawa limiting the American stake in Canada?

There are two aspects to this. New federal regulations governing foreign investment is one. The Province of Saskatchewan's plans to take over the U.S.-dominated potash industry is another.

Direct U.S. investment in Canada amounts to more than 26 billion dollars, and there is as much again in portfolio investment. More than half of Canada's manufacturing is controlled by Americans, and in some sectors—petroleum, chemicals, autos—the percentage is even higher.

There are many reasons why American investment is so big. A high Canadian tariff wall, for example, persuaded many U.S. firms to build branch plants in Canada. So Canadians feel exploited by American industry, and describe themselves as "hewers of wood and drawers of water."

You hear more and more Canadians saying they are willing to sacrifice their high standard of living to reduce American influence. One day in the not-too-distant future, Canadians may have to put up or shut up on that point.

At present, Government policy is to require foreign investment to be of "significant benefit" to Canada. While that is a shadowy yardstick, the Government so far has been relatively liberal. Complaints from the U.S. are rare. But the mere fact that the screening process is there serves as a disincentive—psychologically, at least—to foreign investors.

The potash case is quite different, but its effect has been quite chilling on the over-all investment climate. Saskatchewan wanted a bigger slice of the potash pie in terms of royalties and taxes. The industry hung back on expansion because of uncertainties about future profitability. Rather than engage in prolonged negotiation or court proceedings, the provincial government decided to take over a controlling share of the industry.

This action at the provincial level was hardly welcomed by Ottawa, which itself was under fire because of its restraints on investment.

Are the Canadians tougher on American investors than on other foreigners?

The fact that the American presence is larger than anyone else's creates the impression it is the prime, if not the only, target. In some cases, that's true. When Canada talks about curbing oil and gas exports, for example, it doesn't make much difference how nondiscriminatory the legislation is. The U.S. is Canada's only customer. But so far, Americans have not been singled out per se.

Do you believe American investment in Canada is slowing down?

Definitely. Basically, a nation can't start screening foreign investments and grabbing off potash mines and expect outsiders to keep on pouring money in. Also, some American subsidiaries in Canada don't need funds from the U.S. They're generating their own new investment capital.

Another point: Canada is no longer an economic hot spot. Labor costs in manufacturing, once well below those in the U.S., now are as high—even higher in some cases. Canada's inflation rate is higher, but its productivity is lower than in the United States. It costs more to borrow money in Canada. And Ottawa's anti-inflation program—with its curbs on company profits and dividends—plus the official warning that the free-market system is not working and that more Government intervention may be inevitable, all dampen interest in Canada.

The impact is obvious. The deficit between the amount of direct capital investment entering Canada and the amount leaving it could reach half a billion dollars this year.

Are Canadian industries moving to the U.S.? Or investing money in America rather than at home?

Yes, to both questions—and for the same reason that Americans and other foreigners are so skeptical about Canada. The grass looks greener elsewhere.

Ahead: Conflict, But No Trade War

Is a Canadian-U.S. mini trade war possible?

Canada's reliance on marketing boards to control agricultural production makes conflict all but inevitable. But there won't be a trade war. There'll be skirmishes—on beef, eggs, agricultural products of all kinds. But even a little war would be harmful to the economies of both countries. And Ottawa knows that, in the end, it would lose.

What about Canada's breaking its trade ties with the U.S. and trying for prosperity through closer relations with the European Common Market? [For additional discussion of this subject, see "Canada and the European Communities," in this section, below.]

That's unimaginable. There's no Canadian politician of any party who seriously believes that could be done. And you can say the same for even the most ardent nationalist.

Of course, Canada and the Common Market have just signed what Ottawa calls a "contractual link" setting up the framework for closer economic co-operation. But no one really knows what will result from the arrangement. Remember, too, that there's little chance the Common Market itself would reach any kind of trade arrangement with Canada that would jeopardize Western Europe's more important ties with the U.S.

Why does Ottawa complain so bitterly about excessive U.S. pressure to influence Canadian foreign policy?

You don't hear that complaint too loudly now. In fact, there has been far more complaining in Washington about Canada's reluctance to back American positions.

One thing that really upsets Ottawa is the "extraterritoriality" exercised under which American subsidiaries in Canada are held liable for violating American laws even when their actions are legal in Canada. Canadian trade with Cuba, for example, is completely legal. But if U.S. subsidiaries in Canada participate, they can be charged with violating America's Trading with the Enemy Act. However, Washington has been more liberal in its policies in this area recently, and the issue of extraterritoriality is no longer the irritant it was a year ago.

What specific policy differences create friction?

Cuba still is probably the major area of difference. But Canadian officials expect new U.S. initiatives toward Fidel Castro. . . . Any warming up of U.S.-Cuban relations will immediately soothe the irritations that vex both Washington and Ottawa.

A further point: Ottawa wants no part of the "confrontation" policy the U.S. occasionally pursues—the threat to intervene in Angola, or invade an oil-producing country in the Middle East in the event of another boycott. Also, Canada considers itself a kind of bridge between the industrialized West and the "third world," and in the American view often seems to come down too much on the side of the nonaligned nations. But it would be an exaggeration to say this is a matter of critical concern in either capital.

Do Canadians complain about the cost of belonging to the North Atlantic Treaty Organization?

Sure they complain, but not very loudly. The cost of membership in NATO will hardly bankrupt the country. Canada, in fact, ranks near the bottom of the list in per capita spending on the NATO forces.

Some Canadians maintain the contribution is so small and meaningless that Ottawa should scrub the effort. Most

Canadians won't buy that argument. Others urge that Ottawa drastically increase its contribution to the Alliance. That's not likely, either. So even though Ottawa will have to spend billions to modernize its military forces, there will be no dramatic changes in its contribution to the Allied defense effort.

What about U.S.-Canadian defense ties? Are they solid?

As I said earlier, the U.S. manages to avoid being too critical. As a result, both Canadian and U.S. officials say their joint-defense relations are sound. Canada's major job is to help spot and then intercept any manned-bomber attacks from the Far North and to conduct antisubmarine surveillance in the North Atlantic.

How does Canada plan to patrol and protect its 200-mile maritime economic zone?

That's a big question mark. Critics contend it will be impossible, given the country's weak air arm and thin naval forces. Even now, Canada does a poor job of patrolling its own Far North. Guarding the new economic zone at sea would be more difficult.

What Ottawa is trying to do is reach bilateral agreements with countries whose fishermen normally have operated inside the 200-mile economic zone. This would head off confrontations. But if there should be wide-scale violations, Canada undoubtedly would have to upgrade its patrol forces.

"Tough Bargaining" Over Sea Rights

Do Canadians see conflicts with the U.S. over fishing and mineral interests in adjoining sea areas?

There's probably going to be some tough bargaining ahead. Salt-water boundaries never have been drawn beyond the 3-mile limits off the East and West Coasts and in the Arctic. There are conflicting claims as to who owns Machias Seal Island off Maine. Fishing disputes have often been bitter. And if gas, oil and other minerals are discovered in abundance in any of the disputed areas, the "unique relationship" will face a rough test.

Looking ahead—say, to 1980—do you anticipate more cooperation or sharper conflict between the U.S. and Canada?

If Canada continues to pursue its "separate identity"—as now seems almost certain—there are bound to be more irritations, more disputes, and many will be heated. Some issues could even get out of hand and set off retaliation by one side or the other.

Cool heads will be needed. But ties between the two countries are so close, their desire to remain friends so strong, the need to preserve the relationship so great, that it's hard to see any major disaster on the horizon.

Americans could count themselves fortunate if all their troubles with other countries should be like those between the U.S. and Canada.

CANADA: BEEFING UP ITS DEFENSE [3]

Reprinted from *U.S. News & World Report.*

Canada has decided to modernize its armed forces with a multibillion-dollar facelift, in contrast to foot-dragging by most Atlantic Alliance partners.

Except for West Germany, the European Allies are cutting defense spending, even though their adversaries—the Soviet-led Warsaw Pact nations—are building up their military muscle and creating tensions.

Ottawa's new program—which could eventually cost close to 6 billion dollars—will add punch to Canada's 5,000-man NATO [North Atlantic Treaty Organization] force in Western Europe, strengthen its antisubmarine air patrols over the North Atlantic and permit closer surveillance of its own vast Arctic regions.

[3] From news report entitled "Canada: One Ally That's Beefing Up Its Defense." *U.S. News & World Report.* 80:81-2. F. 16, '76.

Vanished Fears

The decision to step up military spending, moreover, puts to rest fears that Canada intended to abandon a land role in NATO in favor of an all-air contribution as a prelude to total withdrawal. This could have led to unraveling of the Alliance and thrust the responsibility for Western Europe's defense almost entirely into the hands of the U.S. and West Germany.

Also muted—but not entirely stilled—is criticism within Canada that neglect and obsolete equipment had turned the armed forces into a powder-puff military machine that would be hard-pressed to defend Canada, much less help protect Western Europe.

Military analysts have accused Canada of taking a "free ride" on the backs of the U.S. and European Allies. Even the head of Canada's Maritime Command, with some of his ships idled for lack of funds, declared it was time for the nation to put up or shut up about its ability to protect itself.

Expansion Planned

Now Canada has decided to put up. Under its new military blueprint, the Government expects to increase arms spending gradually over the next five years until outlays for planes, tanks and other weapons take at least 20 per cent of the total defense budget. Canada now spends less than 11 per cent of its 2.8-billion-dollar defense budget on armaments.

The plan includes these changes:

☐ Purchase from the U.S., at a cost of nearly 1 billion dollars, 18 P-3 long-range patrol planes with highly sophisticated electronic gear. They will replace 26 aging Argus aircraft now used for "sovereignty protection" and for NATO antisubmarine patrols. Delivery will begin in 1979.

☐ Modernization of Canada's armored force in NATO —now made up of Centurion tanks introduced in 1954— either by refitting 113 Centurions at a cost of 85 million dollars or by purchasing 113 new Leopard tanks from West Germany for 200 million.

☐ Replacement in the early 1980s with a new generation of aircraft of 36 CF-104 Starfighter jets based in Europe and 44 CF-101 Voodoo interceptors deployed with the North American Air Defense Command. The Ministry of National Defense has not yet decided on a replacement jet, although some NATO members have selected the American F-16, with a price of more than 6 million dollars each.

☐ Strengthening of Canadian naval forces at some future time.

None of this will erase overnight Canada's image as a military midget. The nation is a long way from being recognized as a top military power.

The armed forces number only 78,000, with reserves of 20,900. Latest plans call for a 1,100-man increase in the reserves. There will be no jump in the regular military forces. By contrast, the Netherlands, with a population a little more than half of Canada's 23 million, has more than 110,000 men in the armed forces and nearly 100,000 in the reserves.

And even neutral Sweden, a country of 8 million people, has 66,000 in the military, 685,000 in the reserves.

Canada is one of the world's major trading nations. Yet its Navy has only 20 destroyers and destroyer escorts, 3 large support vessels and just 3 conventionally powered submarines. One third of the country lies north of the 60th parallel, but the military does not own a single icebreaker and relies on 23 operated by the Ministry of Transport.

In the mid-1960s, the Air Force had 300 combat planes earmarked for NATO missions alone. Now its combat effectiveness depends mainly on 80 Starfighters and Voodoos. . . .

Widespread Duties

Despite their small numbers, Canada's military men have wide-ranging obligations. A defense white paper issued in 1971 described them this way:

Protection of Canadian sovereignty through surveillance of the land and coast; defense of North America in cooperation with the U.S.; fulfillment of NATO commitments; participation in international peacekeeping.

The size and geography of Canada, the world's second-largest country next to the Soviet Union, makes these duties all the more difficult.

The armed forces are responsible for protecting 3.8 million square miles of Canada itself and for surveillance over 4.7 million square miles of the Arctic, Atlantic and Pacific Oceans as part of domestic, NATO and U.S.-Canadian defense arrangements. Critics of Canada's defense policy charge that Prime Minister Pierre Trudeau, despite these obligations, has shortchanged the armed forces and reduced their combat capabilities. They cite these examples:

Size of the armed forces has dropped from 120,000 men in 1964 to the present 78,000. Canada's contribution to NATO has been halved since Mr. Trudeau took office in 1967, from 10,000 troops to 5,000.

While other NATO countries began replacing their tanks with newer models years ago, Canada has tried to patch up the Centurion, which one officer describes as a "sheer automotive horror." Canada has only 233 tanks—more than half of them in storage. Of 54 Centurions attached to NATO's armored force of more than 6,000 tanks, only 32 are operational.

The Government's military spending dropped from 20 per cent of total federal expenditures in 1966 to 10.7 per cent last year. In 1974, just 2.1 per cent of Canada's gross national product went to the military. Among NATO Allies, only tiny Luxembourg spent less.

Cutback in 1974

The lowest point came in the fall of 1974 when inflation and a revenue pinch forced a drastic cutback in military operations.

Training budgets were pared, and the Arctic "sovereignty flights"—which even in good times averaged just three a month—were temporarily suspended. The East Coast destroyer fleet was limited to six days at sea monthly. Long-range surveillance of the Atlantic was reduced. In one incident in 1975, a Polish fishing vessel spent several days cruising Canada's Northwest Passage undetected until it put into port at Resolute, N.W.T. [Northwest Territories], for supplies.

While no nation challenges Ottawa's rule over its Arctic region, there is in Canada a persistent undercurrent of fear that the U.S. or some other nation may one day test Canada's control, particularly in the Northwest Passage.

Defense always has been troublesome to Canada. While quick to respond in both world wars and the Korean war, it was a different story between wars. In 1936, the military could find only three Bren guns in all of Canada, and there were only 4,000 men in the Army at the outbreak of World War II.

Partners With U.S.

As many Canadian strategists see it, the country faces no direct military threat from outside because of its immense size, its rugged terrain and its geography, with oceans on three sides.

But because Ottawa is convinced that nuclear attack on the United States would inevitably also wreak havoc on Canada, it supports the concept of nuclear deterrence and works with the U.S. in manning joint surveillance and early warning systems.

The latest Canadian moves to improve its military forces do not satisfy everyone. Many Canadians argue that no more funds should be spent on defense because of the sad state of the economy. Others insist additional money should be funneled into security.

Most Canadian officers, however, look beyond criticism at home to military partners overseas.

The big question for Canada, as one general sees it:

"How much does Canada have to put into the defense pot to show we are a responsible ally?"

Canada's answer comes from another ranking commander. "Criticism from our allies no longer is justified," he says. "We're headed back to our previous high professional standards."

CANADA AND THE EUROPEAN COMMUNITIES [4]

A Framework Agreement for Commercial and Economic Cooperation between Canada and the European Communities was signed at Ottawa on July 6 [1976]. The agreement was signed for the Government of Canada by the Honourable Allan J. MacEachen, [former] secretary of state for external affairs of Canada, and for the European Communities by Mr. Max van der Stoel, minister for foreign affairs of the Kingdom of the Netherlands, President in Office of the Council, and by Sir Christopher Soames, vice-president of the Commission of the European Communities. After the signing of the agreement speeches were made by the signatories at a luncheon to mark the occasion. In their speeches the signatories emphasized the importance they attached to the Framework Agreement in the development of a closer and more vigorous relationship between Canada and the European Communities. The agreement reflects the wish of the contracting parties to add a new community dimension to the cordial and extensive relations which already exist between Canada and each of the member states of the European Communities. It will provide a framework and focus for Canada and European Communities' economic cooperation which should lead to increased trade and investment opportunities between the two sides. The implementation of the agreement should in particular

[4] From press release entitled "Framework Agreement for Commercial and Economic Cooperation Between Canada and the European Communities." Canadian Embassy. Public Affairs Division. 1771 N St. N.W. Washington, DC 20036. '76. p 1-2.

facilitate the expansion of industrial cooperation between Canada and Europe.

Among the principal objectives of economic cooperation, which are identified in the agreement, are: the development of Canadian and European industries; the opening up of new sources of supply and markets; the encouragement of technological and scientific progress; the creation of new employment opportunities; the reduction of regional disparities and the protection and improvement of the environment. Certain features of the agreement may be singled out: the agreement reaffirms the two parties' respect for the principles of the GATT [General Agreement on Tariffs and Trade] and confirms their wish to accord each other most-favoured-nation treatment on an equal and reciprocal basis. The contracting parties undertake to promote the development and diversification of their reciprocal trade to the highest possible level by means of commercial cooperation. To this end they shall, in accordance with their respective policies and objectives:

a) cooperate at the international level and bilaterally in solving commercial problems of common interest;

b) use their best endeavours to grant each other the widest facilities for commercial transactions in which one or the other has an interest;

c) take fully into account their respective interests and needs regarding access to and further processing of resources.

The economic cooperation provisions of the agreement, in addition to setting out the objectives of such cooperation, set out some of the means by which these objectives are to be pursued. These include the encouragement and facilitation of broader intercorporate links between their respective industries, especially in the form of joint ventures, increased two-way investment, technological and scientific exchanges, joint cooperation by their private sectors in third countries, and regular exchanges of information on industrial and economic matters.

The agreement and any action taken thereunder shall in no way affect the powers of the member states of the Communities to undertake economic cooperation bilaterally and to conclude, where appropriate, new cooperation agreements with Canada.

The agreement sets up a Joint Cooperation Committee which will have an important role in the activities to be undertaken. The committee will be responsible for promoting and keeping under review the various aspects of commercial and economic cooperation. It will play an instrumental role in developing contacts and promotional activities between the Community and Canadian enterprises and organizations.

The agreement is concluded for an indefinite period but may be terminated by either contracting party after five years, subject to one year's notice.

Finally, a protocol will be signed in Brussels at a later date concerning commercial and economic cooperation between Canada and the European Coal and Steel Community (ECSC). This protocol will stipulate that the provisions of the Framework Agreement signed this day will also apply to the European Coal and Steel Community.

CANADA AND THE THIRD WORLD [5]

The Canadian Involvement

Over 90 per cent of Canada's trade, vital to her high living standard, is with other developed countries, especially the United States. Nor does this situation seem likely to alter greatly. Canada's alliance with the Atlantic powers, and her modest but increasing relations with the Communist countries, are of obvious relevance in creating for

[5] Excerpts from Introduction by Peyton V. Lyon. *Canada and the Third World*; ed. by P. V. Lyon and T. Y. Ismael. Macmillan of Canada/Maclean-Hunter Press. '76. p xiv-xxx. Copyright © 1976 by The Macmillan Company of Canada Limited. Reprinted by permission. Peyton V. Lyon is a professor of political science at Carleton University in Ottawa; Tareq Y. Ismael, a professor of political science at the University of Calgary, Alberta.

Canadians a secure external environment. The vast majority of immigrants to Canada (at least until . . . [1973]) have come from Europe where, along with the United States, Canada possesses the closest historical, cultural, economic and political ties. Relations with Third World countries are not only less extensive but, by any practical test, less essential to Canada.

This is not to suggest that these relations are trivial. Long before Canada maintained diplomatic relations with any of them, except through London, individual Canadians had established their own links as missionaries, traders, investors or tourists, and a modest stream of Third World immigrants was bound for Canada. In the five years 1970–74, Canada sold a yearly average of $882 million worth of goods to Third World aid recipients, and bought from them goods worth an average of $521 million per year. Canadians have become major investors in the Caribbean and parts of Latin America. The thousands of Canadian missionaries serving in the Third World have been joined by many more Canadians in the employ of voluntary agencies, the Canadian International Development Agency (CIDA), or the United Nations. Over seven hundred young volunteers, and a few older ones, are working in the Third World under the sponsorship of the Canadian University Service Overseas (CUSO). In 1971, more than 35,000 Third World citizens entered Canada as landed immigrants; thousands of others, who had come as visitors, were permitted to stay. By 1974, nearly half the continuing immigrant stream of 203,214 originated in Third World countries, a factor in the increasing racial tension in some Canadian cities. [This trend has been continuing through 1976.–Ed.]

Official Canadian relations with the Third World, although starting much later, developed rapidly. The first Canadian diplomatic mission in the area was a legation in Brazil, opened in 1941, and the first High Commission was established in New Delhi in 1947. By 1974 Canada had thirty-eight ambassadors or high commissioners resident in the Third World, and maintained relations with sixty other countries in the area through multiple accreditation. . . .

Development Assistance

Canada's principal involvements in the Third World are now as a peacekeeper and a major participant in international economic development. In 1949 she assisted in setting up the Colombo Plan for economic assistance, largely to [the British] Commonwealth countries in Asia. Subsequently, Canadian aid has been channelled to other areas as well, such as the Caribbean, Africa and Latin America, and through multilateral agencies such as those of the United Nations. The quality of Canadian aid, including many of the terms on which it is granted, compares favourably with the aid of other donors; the ratio of grants to loans, for example, is exceptionally high; a large portion of the loans bear no interest and are repayable over fifty years with an initial ten years of grace. These terms are softer than those of almost any other donor and mean that the grant element in the Canadian loans is about 90 per cent. . . .

Canada's most imaginative initiative in the development field was the establishment in 1970 of the International Development Research Centre. Although its board is international, and its charter permits outside financing, its total budget ($22.6 million in 1973–74) has thus far been provided by Canada. The Centre assists the developing countries to apply science and technology to their problems primarily as *they* define them, and most of its research takes place in the Third World. Another instance of Canadian pioneering is in collaborating with non-governmental organizations (NGO's). These are especially effective in social development, and about half the $30 million spent by CIDA in support of Canadian NGO's goes for this purpose; another third goes to education. Although government financing of private agencies, especially church groups, can give rise to domestic political controversy, the experiment appears highly successful. . . .

Peacekeeping

Canada's most prominent involvement in the Third World has been her enthusiastic support of peacekeeping operations, all of which have occurred in this area. She became an active peacekeeper for reasons very different from those that explain her support of international development. While initially her foreign aid was largely a manifestation of her attachment to the Commonwealth, especially her desire to assist the United Kingdom meet its postwar financial obligations, Canada became the world's most ardent peacekeeper through her concern about global security and her extraordinary commitment to the United Nations; no country has been more consistent or generous in its support of the world organization. However, while her original motivations were different, Canada now supports U.N. peacekeeping for much the same reasons as those for which she supports international development.

Canada has supplied troops for all the U.N. peacekeeping operations of any significance; in the process she has gained more first-hand knowledge about their modalities, possibilities and limitations than any other country. . . .

Canada also helped man the three ICSC's (International Commissions for Supervision and Control, often referred to as ICC's), tripartite teams set up by the Geneva Conference of 1954 to observe the "peace" in Vietnam, Cambodia and Laos; at the peak of their activity in 1955, 170 Canadians, one-seventh of whom were professional diplomats, were engaged on these Commissions. By their disbandment in 1973, the total had dwindled to 15. In the same year, however, Canada sent out 290 diplomatic and military personnel to form part of the quadrapartite ICCS (International Commission for Control and Supervision) agreed to under the Paris accord for Vietnam that was negotiated in late 1972. These were withdrawn in July 1973, and the Canadians were replaced by Iranians. The United Nations bore responsibility for neither the tripartite ICSC's (Canada, India, Poland) nor the quadrapartite (Canada, Hungary, Indonesia, Poland) ICCS.

In 1964, the peak year of peacekeeping activity, 2,122 Canadians were serving under the United Nations flag or with the ICSC's in Indochina. By September 1975, the number was down to 1,547, still the largest national component of the 8,673 men serving the United Nations as keepers of the peace. . . .

The outstanding contribution made by Canadian soldiers and officials to successive U.N. missions in the field has been matched by the endeavours of Canadian politicians and diplomats to negotiate the establishment of peacekeeping operations, generally under emergency conditions, and also to place the entire function on a less ad hoc basis. . . .

No other nation has done as much as Canada to convert the United Nations into an effective instrument for the containment of local disturbances by the interposition of international forces designed to police truce agreements and inhibit the intrusion of other nations, especially the super powers. This activity, a source of pride to many Canadians, has helped generate a sense of distinctive national identity. It has also served to make Canadians more aware of the Third World. Although clearly less naïve in its expectations, the Canadian public in . . . [1976] still appears firm in its general support of the peacemaking function.

Race and Commonwealth

For most Africans at least, the acid test of a white, developed nation's sensitivity to the contents of the Third World has become its stand on the issues of racial injustice and lingering colonialism. Canada's record in this sphere has been mixed; it is not yet clear that she will pass the test. In the United Nations, she has become less inhibited about supporting resolutions designed to apply pressure on governments that practise harsh racial discrimination against their black majorities. . . .

The bulk of Canada's external aid has gone to India and Pakistan. Partly for this reason, she has been compelled to concern herself with the disputes over Kashmir and Bangladesh, but this involvement has occasioned relatively little controversy within Canada. The situation with respect to Indochina is different; while little aid . . . [was] sent, Canada's long and frustrating membership on the . . . control commissions imposed strains on her relations with other countries, notably India and the United States; it also tended to discredit her external activity in the eyes of many of her own people, some of whom concluded, wrongly, that Canada had become an accomplice in American aggression. The attempted secession of Biafra [in 1966], and Ottawa's reluctance to act contrary to the wishes of the Nigerian government, was another of the relatively few instances when relations with countries in the Third World caused acute controversy within Canada.

In spite of the variations noted above, Canada's involvement in the Third World remains primarily that of an affluent, secure nation with countries enduring poverty, instability and, too often, open conflict. She is widely perceived as inoffensive and well-intentioned. While rightly considered by Arab countries to be pro-Israel, and suspect for different reasons in some Caribbean circles, Canada's involvement in the Third World is generally welcome. Most often it is actively solicited. Her close associations with the United States, and membership in NATO [North Atlantic Treaty Organization], are rarely, if ever, a handicap. On occasion they may even prove to be an advantage; Canada has interested the decision-making elites of Third World countries in good part because she is believed to be both sympathetic to their aspirations and in possession of exceptional access to the major capitals of the western world. On balance, the benefits gained by Canada through alliance participation has probably made it easier for her to contribute to U.N. peacekeeping, military training in developing countries, and other forms of development assistance. She has no imperial tradition to live down, and her relations with Third World countries have been at least as easy and as warm as those of any other developed nation.

BIBLIOGRAPHY

An asterisk (*) preceding a reference indicates that the article or a part of it has been reprinted in this book.

BOOKS AND PAMPHLETS

Abella, I. M. Nationalism, communism and Canadian labour. University of Toronto Press. '73.

Aitchison, J. H. The political process in Canada. University of Toronto Press. '63.

Axline, W. A. and others, eds. Continental community?: independence and integration in North America. McClelland & Stewart. '74.

Balawyder, Aloysius. Canadian-Soviet relations between the world wars. University of Toronto Press. '72.

Beaton, Leonard. The strategic and political issues facing America, Britain and Canada. National Planning Association. 1606 New Hampshire Ave. N.W. Washington, DC 20009. '71.

Bohne, Harald and Pluscauskas, Martha, eds. Subject guide to Canadian books in print, 1973. University of Toronto Press. '74.

Boydell, C. L. ed. Critical issues in Canadian society. Holt. '71.

Brebner, J. B. Canada: a modern history. University of Michigan Press. '70.
New edition revised and enlarged by D. C. Masters.

Cameron, D. R. Nationalism, self-determination and the Quebec Question. Macmillan of Canada. '74.

Canada. Statistics. Canadian Information Division. Canada year book; an annual review of economic, social and political developments in Canada. Information Canada. Ottawa, Ont. K1A 0S9.
Published under the authority of the Minister of Industry, Trade and Commerce.

Canadian-American Committee. Keeping options open in Canada-U.S. and natural gas trade. Canadian-American Committee. 1606 New Hampshire Ave. N.W. Washington, DC 20009. '75.

*Canadian-American Committee. A time of difficult transitions: Canada-U.S. relations in 1976. C. D. Howe Research Institute.

2060 Sun Life Bldg. Montreal, Que. H3B 2X7. Canada; National Planning Association. 1606 New Hampshire Ave. N.W. Washington, DC 20009. '76.

*Canadian Embassy. Public Affairs Division. Framework agreement for commercial and economic cooperation between Canada and the European communities [press release]. The Embassy. 1771 N St. N.W. Washington, DC 20036. '76.

*Canadian Embassy. Public Affairs Division. Patriating the British North America Act. (Press Release no. 36) The Embassy. 1771 N St. N.W. Washington, DC 20036. '76.

Cornell, P. G. Canada: unity in diversity. Holt. '70.

Craig, G. M. The United States and Canada. Harvard University Press. '68.

Cuff, R. D. and Granatstein, J. L. Canadian-American relations in wartime: from the Great War to the cold war. Hakkert (Toronto). '75.

Davis, Morris and Krauter, J. F. The other Canadians: profiles of six minorities. Methuen. '71.

Dickey, J. S. and Shepardson, W. H. Canada and the American presence: the U.S. interest in an independent Canada. (Council on Foreign Relations Book) New York University Press. '75.
   Review. Political Science Quarterly. 91:548-50. Fall '76. A. B. Fox.

Dosman, E. J. ed. The Arctic in question. Oxford University Press. '76.

Economic Council of Canada. Looking outward. Information Canada. Ottawa, Ont. K1A 0S9. '75.

Elizabeth II, Queen of Great Britain. Speech from the throne opening the second session of the thirtieth parliament. Canadian Embassy. Public Affairs Division. 1771 N St. N.W. Washington, DC 20036. '76.

Emerick, K. F. War resisters Canada: the world of the American military-political refugees. Knox, Pennsylvania Free Press. P.O. Box 399. Knox, PA 16232. '72.

English, H. E. ed. Canada-United States relations. Praeger. '76.

Finlay, J. L. Canada in the North Atlantic Triangle; two centuries of social change. Oxford. '75.

Fox, A. B. and others, eds. Canada and the United States: transnational and transgovernmental relations. Columbia University Press. '76.

Fry, M. G. ed. "Freedom and change": essays in honour of Lester B. Pearson. McClelland & Stewart. '75.

Glazebrook, G. P. de T. A history of Canadian external relations. (Carleton Library, no 27, 28) McCelland & Stewart. '70-'71. 2v.

Gordon, R. L. Coal and Canada-U.S. energy relations. Canadian-American Committee. 1606 New Hampshire Ave. N.W. Washington, DC 20009. '76.

Harris, R. S. A history of higher education in Canada 1663-1960. University of Toronto Press. '76.

Heap, J. L. ed. Everybody's Canada. Burns & MacEachern. '74.

Hockin, T. A. Government in Canada. Norton. '76.

Hodgetts, J. E. The Canadian public service: a physiology of government, 1867-1970. The University of Toronto Press. '74.

Holmes, J. W. The better part of valour: essays on Canadian diplomacy. (Carleton Library no 49) McClelland & Stewart. '70.

Horowitz, Gad. Canadian labour in politics. University of Toronto Press. '73.

Hughes, E. C. French Canada in transition. University of Chicago Press. '63.

Hunt, C. B. Natural regions of the United States and Canada. Freeman. '73.

Hutchison, Bruce. The far side of the street. Macmillan of Canada. '76.
    A reporter on Canada's political leaders.

Jamieson, Donald. Notes for a speech to the United Nations General Assembly, New York, September 29, 1976. Canadian Embassy. Public Affairs Division. 1771 N St. N.W. Washington, DC 20036. '76.

Kasinsky, R. G. Refugees from militarism: draft-age Americans in Canada. Transaction Books. '76.

Kornberg, Allan and Mishler, William. Influence in parliament: Canada. Duke University Press. '76.

Krueger, R. R. and Bryfogle, R. C. comps. Urban problems: a Canadian reader. Holt. '71.

Kunz, F. A. The modern senate of Canada, 1925-1963; a re-appraisal. University of Toronto Press. '65.

Lang, G. E. ed. Canada. (Reference Shelf, v 31 no 4) Wilson. '59.

*Lyon, P. V. and Ismael, T. Y. eds. Canada and the third world. Macmillan of Canada/Maclean-Hunter Press. '76.
    Reprinted in this book: excerpts from Introduction. P. V. Lyon. p xiv-xxx.

Lyon, Peter, ed. Britain and Canada: survey of a changing relationship. Cass. '76.

McNaught, K. W. K. The history of Canada. Praeger. '70.

McNaught, K. W. K. The Pelican history of Canada. Penguin. '69.

Mallory, J. R. The structure of Canadian government. rev ed Macmillan. '74.

Mandel, E. W. comp. Contexts of Canadian criticism. University of Chicago Press. '71.

Maxwell, Judith. Energy from the Arctic: facts and issues. Canadian-American Committee. c/o National Planning Association. 757 Sun Life Bldg. Montreal, Que. H3B 2X7. Canada. '73.

Mickenberg, N. H. ed. Native rights in Canada. 2d ed Ontario. General Publishing Company. '72. [Published for the Indian-Eskimo Association of Canada, Toronto]

Moffett, S. E. The Americanization of Canada. University of Toronto Press. '72.

Morris, R. A. and Lanphier, M. C. Individual, collective and cultural inequalities: perspectives on French-English relations. Longman Canada Limited. '76.

Morton, W. L. The Canadian identity. 2d ed. University of Wisconsin Press. '72.

National Film Board of Canada. Between friends/Entre amis. McClelland & Stewart. '76.
Official gift from Canadian people to their US neighbors on the 200th anniversary of the US Declaration of Independence.
Excerpt: Between friends: the U.S./Canadian border. Reader's Digest. 109:196-204. N. '76.

Ossenberg, R. J. ed. Canadian society: pluralism, change and conflict. Prentice-Hall of Canada. '71.

Park, Julian, ed. The culture of contemporary Canada. Cornell University Press. '57.

Penniman, H. R. ed. Canada at the polls: the general election of 1974. American Enterprise Institute for Public Policy Research. 1150 17th St. N.W. Washington, DC 20036.

Presthus, R. V. Elite accommodation in Canadian politics. Cambridge. '73.

Preston, R. A. ed. The influence of the United States on Canadian development. Duke University Press. '72.

Reid, J. H. S. and others. A source-book of Canadian history. Longmans. '59.

Rioux, Marcel and Martin, Yves, eds. French-Canadian society. (Carleton Library no 18) McClelland & Stewart. '71.

Rotstein, Abraham and Lax, Gary, comps. Independence: the Canadian challenge. McClelland & Stewart. '72. [Published for the Committee for an Independent Canada]

Schwartz, M. A. Politics and territory: the sociology of regional persistence in Canada. McGill-Queens University Press. '74.

Simeon, R. E. B. Federal-provincial diplomacy: the making of recent policy in Canada. University of Toronto Press. '72.

Taylor, Charles. Snow job: Canada, the United States and Vietnam (1954 to 1973). Books Canada, Inc. 33 E. Tupper St. Buffalo, NY 14203. '74.

Teeple, Gary, ed. Capitalism and the national question in Canada. University of Toronto Press. '72.

Thomson, D. C. ed. Quebec society and politics: views from the inside. McClelland & Stewart. '73.

Wade, Mason. The French Canadians, 1760-1967. rev ed St. Martin's. '68. 2v.

Walz, Jay and Walz, Audrey. Portrait of Canada. (A New York Times Book) American Heritage. '70.

Williams, R. N. The new exiles: American war resisters in Canada. Liveright. '71.

Wonders, W. C. ed. The north. University of Toronto Press. '72. [published for the 22d International geographical congress]

Woodcock, George. Canada and the Canadians. 2d ed rev Faber. '73.

Zureik, Elia and Pike, R. M. eds. Socialization and values in Canadian society. McCelland & Stewart. '75. 2v.
  v 1: Political socialization. v 2: Socialization, social stratification, and ethnicity.

PERIODICALS

*Academy of Political Science. Proceedings. v 32, no 2:1-180. '76. Canada-United States relations. H. E. English, ed.
  Reprinted in this volume: Quebec and the bicultural dimension. D. C. Thomson. p 27-39.

*American Libraries. 6:24-7. Ja. '75. Canadian conundrums. Mordecai Richler.

Atlantic. 232:81-2+. Jl. '73. The strangers next door. Edith Iglauer.
  Discussion. Atlantic. 232:31-2+. S. '73.

Atlantic Community Quarterly. 12:358-70. Fall '74. Canada's industrial policy. André Raynauld.

Better Homes & Gardens. 52:115-20. S. '74. What to see and do in Canada's great cities. G. G. Greer.

Canadian Geographical Journal. 92:4-13. Ja. '76. American impact upon Canada. Kenneth McNaught.

Canadian Geographical Journal. 92:30-5. Mr. '76. Canada's role in American history. G. M. Craig.

Canadian Historical Review. 57:115-31. Mr. '76. Recent publications relating to Canada. Murray Barkley.

Canadian Journal of Political Science. 8:40-62. Mr. '75. Canada and the quest for a national policy. D. V. Smiley.

Canadian Journal of Political Science. 9:227-43. Je '76. A reinterpretation of Canadian-American relations. J. H. Redekop.

Christian Century. 91:800-2. Ag. 21, '74. Canada and world population: attitudes and approaches. Claude De Mestral.

Chronicle of Higher Education. 13:5. N. 29, '76. Struggle over who runs Canada complicates university financing. P. W. Semas.

Current Biography. 29:38-41. N. '68. Pierre Elliott Trudeau.
    Also in: Current Biography Yearbook 1968:404-7. '69.

Current Biography. 36:26-8. Ja. '75. René Lévesque.
    Also in: Current Biography Yearbook 1975:241-3. '76.

Current Biography. 37:3-6. S. '76. (Jean) Robert Bourassa.

Current History. 66:145-81+. Ap. '74. Canada, 1974, symposium.

Department of State Bulletin. 73:633-43. N. 3, '75. Secretary of State Kissinger visits Canada; exchange of remarks, toasts, and transcript of news conference, October 14 and 15, 1975. A. J. MacEachen; H. A. Kissinger.

Economist. 261:15-16. N. 20, '76. Canada's last chance.

Esquire. 85:24-5. My. '76. There's more to Canada than just east or west. Richard Joseph.

Esquire. 85:86-8+. My. '76. Who would have thought there was so much to do up in Canada? Richard Joseph.

Forces. no 34/35:81-4. 1er and 2e trimestres. '76. Quebec, gateway to North America. J. Sarrazin.

Forces. no 34/35:88-90. 1er and 2e trimestres. '76. Montreal, North America's transportation hub. J. C. Lassère.

*Foreign Affairs. 54:734-44. Jl. '76. For an independent Québec. René Lévesque.

*Foreign Affairs. 55:97-118. O. '76. Canada: the new nationalism. Abraham Rotstein.

*Fortune. 94:179-83+. Ag. '76. Canada's nationalism exacts a high price. H. E. Meyer.

Geographic Magazine. 48:136-7+. D. '75. Even Canada has an energy problem. W. R. D. Sewell and H. D. Foster.

Green Revolution. August 1976 issue. Canada—alternative to the north? Paul Salstrom, ed.

*Harper's Magazine. 250:28-32. Je. '75. Letter from Ottawa: the sorry state of Canadian nationalism. Mordecai Richler.

Harvard Business Review. 51:69-79. S. '73. Canada's declaration of less dependence. J. D. Gibson.

Industrial Relations. 15:295-312. O. '76. Canada-U.S. labor link under stress. J. R. Grodin.

International Journal. 30:384-98. Spring '75. The Canadian military and the use of force: end of an era? R. B. Byers.

International Organization. 28:595-1023. Autumn '74. Canada and the United States: transnational and transgovernmental relations; ed. by A. B. Fox and others [symposium].

International Perspectives (Journal of the Department of External Affairs, Ottawa). p 29-37. N./D. '75. The myth and reality of Canada-U.S. relations. Irving Brecher.

Journal of Canadian Studies. 11:1-2+. F. '76. A royal commission on urban design. Ralph Heintzman.

Library Journal. 100:802+. My. 1, '75. Canada cracks down on sale of U.S. books and magazines.

*Maclean's. 88:25-9. My. '75. Land grab. Harry Bruce.

Maclean's. 89:54. My. 17, '76. If it's French-without-tears, why isn't it French-without-opposition? Julianne Labreche.

Maclean's. 89:28-32. Je. 28, '76. Bulldozers Inc. Walter Stewart.

Maclean's. 89:18-20. Jl. 12, '76. Canada: a nation divided against itself. Robert Lewis.

Maclean's. 89:26-8+. S. 6, '76. Quebec: a report on the state of a nation. Mark Nichols.

Maclean's. 89:53. S. 20, '76. Feed the world's starving millions? We may not be able to feed our own. Terence Dickinson.

*Maclean's. 89:22-4. O. 4, '76. The return of a man called Trudeau. Ian Urquhart.

Maclean's. 89:18-22. N. 1, '76. A terminal failure to communicate?

Maclean's. 89:42m-p. N. 15, '76. Canada-U.S. relations: the five main issues. Walter Stewart.

*Nation. 220:722-4. Je. 14, '75. Reverse invasion: the Canadians are coming! M. A. Kellogg.

National Geographic. 148:190-215. Ag. '75. Canada's dowager [Toronto] learns to swing. E. A. Starbird.

National Geographic. 150:480-511. O. '76. Canada's "now" frontier. R. P. Jordan.

New York Times, sec III, p 1. Ag. 1, '76. Imperial oil's ills: as big as Canada. Paul Lewis.

New York Times. p 7. Ag. 22, '76. Canada debates immigration ideas. Robert Trumbull.

New York Times. p 49. Ag. 25, '76. Canadian bankers cautiously welcome revisions to bank act. Robert Trumbull.

*New York Times. p E 3. Ag. 29, '76. Canada: more at stake than the language. Robert Trumbull.

New York Times. p 43+. S. 2, '76. U.S. tourist drop upsets Canada. Robert Trumbull.

New York Times. p 13. S. 27, '76. Indians in Alberta have friend at top. Robert Trumbull.

New York Times. p E 4. O. 10, '76. The Great Lakes have a new enemy: the air. Gladwin Hill.

New York Times. p 3. O. 26, '76. Indians ask Canada for a province.

*New York Times. p 3. O. 26, '76. Language dispute is termed threat to Canada's unity. Robert Trumbull.

New York Times. p 2. N. 18, '76. Election divisions in Montreal. Henry Giniger.

New York Times. p 13. N. 21, '76. Uneasy Canada tries to decipher Quebec election. Robert Trumbull.

*New York Times. p E 2. N. 21, '76. How Canada is governed.

*New York Times. p E 2. N. 21, '76. An uneasy alliance: Canada and its provinces. Henry Giniger.

New York Times. p 2. N. 22, '76. Independence referendum promised by Quebec leader. Henry Giniger.

New York Times. p 25. N. 22, '76. 54-40 and no fight. William Safire.

New York Times. p E 15. N. 28, '76. A sudden problem in the north. Tom Wicker.

New York Times Magazine. p 18-19+. Ap. 21, '74. Canada wants out [of the United States]. Robert Fulford.

*New York Times Magazine. p 40-1+. Je. 6, '76. Waking up from the Canadian dream. Gerald Clark.

*Newsweek. 88:41-2. N. 29, '76. Québec, oui. Raymond Carroll, with Jon Lowell.

Orbis. 18:582-93. Summer '74. Stresses and fractures in Canadian-American relations: the emergence of a new environment. G. F. Rutan.

Public Administration Review. 33:1-51. Ja. '73. Canadian public administration. E. F. Ricketts, ed.

*Ramparts. 13:40-4. Mr. '75. The Canadian way: no exit? E. Z. Friedenberg.

Saturday Review. 4:44-5. O. 16, '76. In English-French Canada, dance is the common tongue. Walter Terry.

Saturday Review/World. 1:16+. My. 18, '74. Canadians are reclaiming Canada. Valerie Miner.

Senior Scholastic. 102:5-8+. My. 7, '73. Canada and its identity [special issue].

Senior Scholastic. 107:14-15. O. 7, '75. Canada: seeking a national identity.

Sociology and Social Research. 59:163-70. Ja. '75. Canadians' and Americans' national impressions. B. I. Silverman and Shelly Battram.

Time. 107:32. Mr. 22, '76. Trudeau's troubles.

Times Literary Supplement. 72:1295-6. O. 26, '73. Canada's Elizabethan age? Ronald Sutherland.

*U.S. News & World Report. 77:39-40+. O. 28, '74. Canada to U. S. on oil: we'll meet our own needs first [interview]. D. S. Macdonald.

U.S. News & World Report. 79:68. Jl. 7, '75. Bilingualism in Canada: still a distant goal.

*U.S. News & World Report. 80:81-2. F. 16, '76. Canada: one ally that's beefing up its defense.

*U.S. News & World Report. 81:69-70+. O. 18, '76. Why friend-
    ship has cooled between U.S. and Canada [interview]. Gerson
    Yalowitz.
U.S. News & World Report. 81:48-52. D. 31, '76. Tragedy of the
    "two Canadas." K. M. Chrysler.
Village Voice. p 81. Ag. 16, '76. Canada's national arts center does
    almost everything right. Leighton Kerner.
Vital Speeches of the Day. 42:588-94. Jl. 15, '76. Canada and the
    United States; address, April 29, 1976. J. H. Warren.
*Wall Street Journal. p 42. O. 18, '76. Another Alaskan pipeline
    is in the works as the U.S., Canada, mull a joint venture. Tim
    Metz.
Washington Post. p B-5. S. 21, '76. Now Calgary has an Aurora
    Borealis to call its own. Richard Van Abbe.
*Washington Post. p A-19. O. 19, '76. An inflationary lesson from
    Canada. Joseph Kraft.
Wilson Library Bulletin. 51:67-71. S. '76. Libraries in the Cana-
    dian mosaic. W. R. Eshelman.
Working Papers for a New Society. 4:26-9. Summer '76. Making
    work. T. A. Barocci.
World Politics. 29:29-66. O. '76. Foreign policy decision making:
    the case of Canada and nuclear weapons. H. H. Lentner.
World Today. 32:376-86. O. '76. Canada and Latin America. J. J.
    Guy.